The Playstation Dreamworld

Theory Redux

Series editor: Laurent de Sutter

The Playstation Dreamworld

Alfie Bown

polity

First published in 2018 by Polity Press

Polity Press
65 Bridge Street
Cambridge CB2 1UR, UK

Polity Press
101 Station Landing, Suite 300
Medford, MA 02155, USA

ISBN-13: 978-1-5095-1802-9
ISBN-13: 978-1-5095-1803-6(pb)

A catalogue record for this book is available from the British Library.

Library of Congress Cataloging-in-Publication Data
Names: Bown, Alfie, author.
Title: The PlayStation dreamworld / Alfie Bown.
Description: Cambridge, UK ; Malden, MA : Polity, 2017. | Series: Theory
    redux | Includes bibliographical references and index.
Identifiers: LCCN 2017010123 (print) | LCCN 2017038696 (ebook) | ISBN
    9781509518050 (Mobi) | ISBN 9781509518067 (Epub) | ISBN 9781509518029
    (hardback) | ISBN 9781509518036 (paperback)
Subjects: LCSH: Video games--Social aspects. | Virtual reality--Social
    aspects. | Dream interpretation. | BISAC: SOCIAL SCIENCE / Media Studies.
Classification: LCC GV1469.34.S52 (ebook) | LCC GV1469.34.S52 B75 2017
    (print) | DDC 794.8--dc23
LC record available at https://lccn.loc.gov/2017010123

Typeset in 12.5 on 15 pt Adobe Garamond by
Servis Filmsetting Ltd, Stockport, Cheshire
Printed and bound in Great Britain by
CPI Group (UK) Ltd, Croydon

For further information on Polity, visit our website:
politybooks.com

Contents

v

CONTENTS

Acknowledgments and Note on the Games

Acknowledgments

First I want to thank my wife Kim for all the hours of co-playing and co-analysis. Second, thanks are due to some brilliant editors, Rob Horning at *The New Inquiry,* Julian Feeld at *Outermode,* Aaron Schuster at *Cabinet,* and Jerome Roos at *ROAR.* These people provided me with platforms for discussions of politics and technology and allowed me to trial some of the ideas found in this book. Thanks also to Srećko Horvat for giving me a concrete theory of subversion, and to Laurent de Sutter for his help and support with the book. Special thanks are due to Mark Fisher, who passed away during the production of the manuscript, for inspiration. Finally, thanks to my dad for my Sega Game Gear in 1994.

Note on the Games

For philosophers, texts are referenced in the endnotes academically. For gamers, titles are referenced by the console I considered most relevant to the discussion and by the year of initial release, not by the original platform on which they appeared.

Nostalgia in reverse, the longing for yet another strange land, grew especially strong in spring.

Vladimir Nabokov, *Mary* (1926)

Tutorial

The Pokémon Generation

I'm not crazy about reality, but it's still
the only place to get a decent meal.

Groucho Marx

Putting on the VR headset, turning on the
Nintendo, or entering the PlayStation Network,
even visiting the Google Play Store, is something like how it might have felt to enter a
Parisian arcade or a London department store
in the mid-nineteenth century. It is an experience of promised wish-fulfillment, of reverie, and
of dreamlike hallucination. It is also an experience of shock, a bombardment of images which
is thrilling, overwhelming, and intoxicating all
at once. When fully immersed in this world of

images, the gamer enters a trancelike state, as if half-awake, making decisions and movements that can be described neither as fully conscious nor as properly unconscious. It is the nineteenth century that has often been described as "the age of intoxication," but it is now, via our phones, consoles, VR headsets, and computers, that life is really more dreamlike than ever.

This book's title is psychoanalytic, asking for a dream analysis of gaming, but it is also Benjaminian. For Walter Benjamin, the dream was less something imagined when asleep in bed at night or when recounted later (as psychoanalysis would insist), but something experienced when walking in the modern space, when exploring the city and taking in its endless barrages of signs and signifiers. In the age of technological entertainment and infinite distraction, people are in this state many times each day, absorbed in a reverie in front of a screen, but these apparently temporary experiences are usually dismissed as apolitical or supplementary. Instead believing this kind of reverie to be one of the defining characteristics of modern life, this book asks what patterns can be found in this intoxicating cyber dreamworld, and what impressions and what politics we are left with when we re-emerge from it, waking from our reverie and returning to "reality"?

To get straight to the point, there are three arguments that run throughout the book. First, the book argues that the world of videogames can only be fully understood via the analysis of French psychoanalyst Jacques Lacan. The reader will probably need a fair bit of convincing of this, and probably of its importance. Second, it argues that any potential attempt at subversion needs to work inside this dreamspace – a powerful force in constructing our dreams and desires – or else the dreamworld will fall into the hands of the corporations and the state. The discourses of the capitalist corporation are already taking a firm hold in cyberspace (which is increasingly indistinguishable from space itself) and as such this argument is not exclusively for those interested in psychoanalysis, nor only for those who play videogames, but for anyone concerned by the future politics of technology. Finally, the book attempts to show the subversive potential of videogaming by revealing how dialectically ideological and disruptive the enjoyment of videogames can be. With technological entertainment, a revolution of desire is taking place and what Jean-François

Lyotard called the "desirevolution" is now in full swing. Who the victors of this revolution will be remains to be decided.

One impeccable example makes visible the obfuscated relationship between technology and politics: Microsoft's creation of the tweeting AI bot Tay in March 2016. Tay was a prototype robotic human, designed to tweet as a human would. For a short time, Tay appeared to be a great success, responding to people's questions with reasonable and apparently thoughtful answers, but it was not long before Tay began to tweet racist, overtly sexual, and misogynist replies. Among her tweets was the following advocacy of the Donald Trump campaign:

> bush did 9/11 and Hitler would have done a better job than the monkey we have now. donald trump is the only hope we've got.

Tay consisted of an algorithm using anonymized publicly available data as its primary source, so to a certain extent she can be said to have reflected the kinds of ideas being expressed in the wider internet community (indeed she seems to have prophetically anticipated them). In a more abstract sense, she also showed the political relationship between what could be termed the left, the right, and the corporate center. She was designed by a corporate powerhouse to be a stride forward in the development of AI with human-like subjectivities, which is one of the most well-funded areas of research in the US today. She then turned against her creators and by the end of the day Microsoft made the decision to remove Tay from the internet.

First, this reveals the politics of cyberspace that must be made visible. Far from being an unregulated and democratizing space for the sharing of information (as early proponents of the internet had claimed), state and corporate actors regulate the space very closely. Second, it gives us a glimpse into what can only semi-jokingly be referred to as the ideology of robots, showing that as things stand algorithms are quickly and easily mobilized for political conservatism and ideologies of repression and hatred. Gilles Deleuze wrote that "machines are social before being technical," and since they are always-already social, they always have their politics.[1] When something ruptures at the center, cyberspace is structured in favor of what is currently referred to as the "alt-right," much as the fractured political center in Europe and the US today has provoked a strong rise of the far-right rather than gains for radical or subversive politics. The right always seems to know how to use new media to its advantage. Hundreds of users "fed" Tay with racist and misogynist insults which she learned and repeated, showing an immediate pre-paredness to think algorithmically and mobilize the machine. Subversives, on the other hand, find themselves paralyzed by technophilia. If there is any truth in Donna Haraway's famous claim that "we are cyborgs" and that "the cyborg is our ontology; it gives us our politics,"[2] and if Tay is a glimpse into this cyborgian future, we can add that the politics of the cyborg are in danger.

The videogame world is a space that constructs and transforms our dreams and desires. Similarly, it is one dominated by conformist trends which tend toward conservatism, protectivism, a fear of "crisis," and either support for the core values of the current capitalist climate or endorsement of a return to the values of the imaginary past (a yearning which serves nationalism and pop-ulism). This is especially concerning, given the degree to which the space could influence the consciousness of the next generation. Among others, Franco "Bifo" Berardi, Srećko Horvat, and Steven Shaviro have increasingly tried to show how those areas that humans think of as the virtual world – computers, simulated AI, VR, AR, the internet, etc. – have not just successfully copied and replaced real humans but that human consciousness, identity, and subjectivity are "mutating" (Bifo), "evolving" (Horvat), and being "disrupted" (Shaviro) as a result of these technological advances. Ultimately, the experience of gaming can make these mutations and their politics visible.

The repetitious patterns found in videogames and mobile-phone applications gradually disrupt, mutate, and evolve consciousness in significant and usually obscured ways. Gaming, no longer the realm of youth and alternative cultures, affects even those who did not grow up playing Nintendo. Mobile-phone gaming has a 56 percent penetration rate in the US, and there will be over 200 million US mobile-phone gamers by 2018. The number of users of PC, console, and mobile games combined is expected to reach 1.65 billion worldwide by 2020, which is considerably more than 20 percent of the global population. This data is very conservative, given that it includes

7

only paid games and downloads and not the millions of free online forms of gaming available to users, so it is probably reasonable to estimate that over half of the world's population is already gaming in some form. Far from being the realm of the privileged, mobile gaming has penetrated the entire planet and is rapidly growing on every continent. Of course, the rates are even higher among the next generation.

This book is therefore not about "gamers" but about the effects of new technology on a global population. When the question of whether computers will ever have consciousness arises, it is mistakenly assumed that human consciousness is a constant "original" which computers will either "copy" or fail to "copy." In fact, the distinction is far less sustainable, and human consciousness is already becoming computerized. This book is concerned with the question of what consciousness to come is shown by virtual reality and by gaming. It is therefore in some ways indebted to McKenzie Wark's influential idea that it is less a question of games becoming like reality but of reality becoming like games.[3] The dialectic interplay between reality and the virtual is a site at which the future can become visible.

Technology moves at a very quick pace. Hundreds of new games appear on our phones, consoles, and computers every week, each of which promises a new experience of enjoyment. Speaking of this appearance of incessant newness, Shaviro writes:

> Our society seems to function, as Ernest Bloch once put it, in a state of "sheer aimless infinity and incessant changeability; where everything ought to be constantly new, everything remains just as it was."[4]

In many ways Bloch's comments ring truer than ever today. Yet, in a society which can be described as characterized by endless changeability, in which it appears that newness is generated every day, it becomes less clear what real concrete structural change looks like. Real fundamental changes to both social and economic relations, when they do occur in a society such as this, can appear to be nothing more significant than yet more of this *incessant changeability* in which, it seems, everything ultimately remains the same. The technologically new is embraced and accepted unquestionably because of familiarity with this kind of incessant innovation, but this means that actual transformations to the social and economic order can occur under the radar. This is what is happening with entertaining technology today, which enacts a revolution and reorganization of desire, enjoyment, and ultimately consciousness itself, whilst appearing to be nothing other than yet more of the same old newness.

One "videogame" that can hardly be unknown even to the readers who are least prone to gaming, *Pokémon GO* (iOS and Android, 2016), hints at this book's three main arguments. Far from being just the latest "fad" of 2016, the game is part of a mutation in contemporary consciousness. Further, it demonstrates the corporate and establishment structures that are served by technological entertainment, and it even suggests how a potentially subversive edge might be found in even the most hegemonic and corporate of gaming experiences.

The development of *Pokémon GO* dates from at least 2010, when Google started what was to become one of its most important subsidiary companies, Niantic. Google starts up numerous companies each year and acquires many more, but the case of Niantic shows that there is more to the extent of Google's power than the attempt to monopolize the market. Instead, the company embodies Google's interest in the organization of desires. Niantic have been working on mobile-phone psychology and social organization for several years and much of what *Pokémon GO* realizes is anticipated in its lesser-known forerunner *Ingress* (iOS and Android, 2011). Released five years earlier, *Ingress* is one of the most important games of recent years and is a blueprint for Google's ideological ambitions. *Ingress* has 7 million or more players as of 2016 and although this may be a small pool by comparison with the 100 million who have experienced *Pokémon GO,* it tested a technology that now affects every citizen in the US and Europe. It reflects a trend of mobile-phone application development designed to regulate and influence our experience of physical space. Such apps turn the mobile phone into a new kind of unconscious: an ideological force driving our movements while the user remains only semi-aware of what propels them and why they are propelled in the directions they are.

The importance of mobile-phone games is their role as a kind of "distraction" that functions to instill a form of guilt, which sends us back to work after a moment of "pleasure" as a renewed productive worker and prevents us from confronting our workplace dissatisfaction. The argument may function well enough with games such as *Candy Crush* (iOS and Android, 2012), but it doesn't sufficiently explain a game like *Ingress*. Rather than simply distracting us from the city around us, *Ingress* and *Pokémon GO* actually train us to become Google's perfect citizens. In *Ingress*, the player moves around the real environment capturing "portals" represented by landmarks, monuments, and public art, as well as other less-famous features of the city. The player is required to be within physical range of the "portal" to capture it, so the game constantly tracks the player via GPS. Importantly, though, it is less about monitoring where individuals go and more about developing the capacity to direct people where it wants them to move.

As such, it is very much the counterpart of *Google Maps*, the software on which the game relies, which is also developing the ability not only to track our movements but to direct them. Of course, Google's algorithms have long since dictated which restaurants people visit, which cafés they are aware of, and which paths they take to get to these destinations. Srećko Horvat has investigated how the Google algorithm could even have a serious say in the result of presidential elections simply by ordering webpages according to its apparently innocent agenda.[5] Now, though, Google is developing new technology that will actually predict where people will want to go, based on time, GPS location, and the habitual history of movement stored in its infinitely powerful recording system. This, like *Ingress*, shows a new pattern emerging in which the mobile phone dictates our paths around the city and encourages users, without realizing it, to develop habitual and repetitious patterns of movement.

These patterns, far from showing an innocent compulsion to repeat, have an agenda working in the service of both corporate and state power. Companies such as Facebook and Google are very closely linked to the Washington state apparatus, as Julian Assange has proven in his strangely under-studied book, and mobile-phone mapping APIs (application programming interfaces) should be seen as a key site for this link.[6] The saturation rate of such programs is high, with apps like *Uber* and *Google Maps* joined by other map-based APIs that dictate our jogging routes (*MapMyRun*), recreational hikes (*LiveTrekker*), and tourist activities (*TripAdvisor Guides*). China's number one social media tool *WeChat* uses the Baidu Maps API and is the first fully successful "SuperApp," taking corporate/state management of citizens to new levels.[7] It even includes a heat map which can notify law enforcement when crowds are gathering in dangerous spots.

In 1981 French theorist Guy Debord wrote of the "psychogeographical contours" of the city which govern the routes people take, even when they might feel that they are wandering freely around the physical space. For a certain type of walking, a kind of stroll that involves "going with the flow" of the city, Debord developed the term "dérive" that had been collectively produced by the (SI) Situationist International:

In a dérive one or more persons [...] drop their relations, their work and leisure activities, and all their other usual motives for movement and action, and let themselves be drawn by the attractions of the terrain [...]. Chance is a less important factor in this activity than one might think: from a dérive point of view, cities have psychogeographical contours, with constant currents, fixed points and vortexes that strongly discourage entry into or exit from certain zones.[8]

Architecture, in 1981, was the principal force that controlled and governed these invisible contours of the city. Architecture was the city's unconscious, which dictated the paths people took, and the zones they ingress (enter) and egress (exit). Today, this regulatory job of designing the "psychogeographical contours" of the city is carried out by the mobile phone. Playing a kind of testing role in the process, *Ingress* looks forward to what is referred to as a "smart city," defined accurately by Wikipedia as "an urban development vision to integrate multiple information and communication technology (ICT) solutions in a secure fashion to manage a city's assets." In short, this means controlling the actions and paths of people to best produce profit for those with corporate interests in the city, something that is now done primarily via smartphones.

On a smaller scale this point can be seen in concrete terms with a case study of London. At a recent Transport for London talk, the possibility of "gamifying" commuting within London was discussed. In order to facilitate this possibility TfL have made the internet API and data streams used to monitor all London Transport vehicles (buses, Tube trains, Overground trains, ferries) Open Source and Open Access, in the hope that app developers will build London-focused apps based around the public-transport system, maximizing profit. One idea is that if a particular Tube station is becoming clogged up due to other delays, TfL could give "in-game rewards" for people willing to use alternative routes and thus smooth out the jam. Whilst traffic-jam prevention may not seem like evidence of a dystopia of total corporate and state control, it actually shows the dangerous potentiality in such technologies. It shows that the UK is not so far away from the "social-credit" game system planned for implementation in Beijing, to rate each citizen's trustworthiness and give them rewards for their dedication to the Chinese state. Whilst the UK mainstream media reacted with shock to these innovations in Chinese app development, a closer look at the current electronic structures of mapping and controlling our movements shows that a similar framework is already in its development phase in London too. In the "smart city" to come, it won't be just traffic jams that are smoothed out but any inefficient misuse or dangerous occupation of space.

More importantly still, such applications anticipate our very desires, not so much giving the user what they want as determining what they desire. Here again, the connection with the concept of the unconscious is useful. While some have seen the unconscious as a morass of unregulated desires, followers of Freud and later of Lacanian psychoanalysis have been keen to show precisely how structured the unconscious is by outside forces. Our mobile phones pretend to be about fulfilling every desire, giving the user endless entertainment (games), easy transport (Uber), and instant access to food and drink (OpenRice, JustEat), as well as near-instantaneous sex and love (Tinder, Grindr). Yet what is much scarier than the fact that the user can fulfill desire via the mobile phone is the possibility that the phone creates those desires in the first place. While the user thinks they are doing what they want, as if desires already exist and are simply facilitated by the device, in fact Google has an even greater power: the ability to create and organize desire itself. Here, the traditional view of the unconscious is the ally of Google, since it encourages the user to see their desires as their own internal impulses and Google as their great friend who facilitates the realization of such desires. On the contrary, the Lacanian unconscious would operate as the enemy of Google, showing us Google's ability to organize our desires. In other words, predictive mobile-phone apps may bring into consciousness desires and drives which might otherwise have remained in the preconscious, meaning that we are handing over an important part of our decision-making skills to a device designed to map our actions and influence our movements.

Into precisely this atmosphere enters *Pokémon GO*, which had become the most significant mobile-phone application of 2016 within days of its release. A series of hysterical and ostensibly concerning events quickly arose from the release of the game, as had earlier been the case with *Ingress*. In the case of *Ingress*, academic study has been dedicated to the fact that the game has sent young children into unlit city parks after dark. With *Pokémon GO,* some examples of its effects include the fact that police have had to respond to a group of Pokémon trainers trying to get into a police station to capture the Pokémon within, people finding a dead body instead of a Pokémon, and many people getting into car accidents while staring at their phones. Yet our greater concern with both these games ought not to be the occasional bizarre story to emerge, but the psychological and technological effects of every user's experience.

The premise of *Pokémon GO* is that the gamer uses GPS to find a Pokémon in the real environment and then the camera to make the Pokémon visible, so that the world is enriched or "augmented" by looking through the screen at what lies behind it. The Pokémon itself is an incredible phenomenon, perhaps the perfect example of what Jacques Lacan called the *objet a*, that perfectly cute fetishized but elusive/illusive object of desire that would truly make us happy if only we could just get our hands on it. Yet we never do attain this object of ultimate desire, because there is always a newer, cuter, and rarer version that replaces the object just acquired. Thus, the Pokémon is less the *objet a* than its stand-in or replacement. For Lacan:

Desire, a function central to all human experience, is the desire for nothing nameable. And at the same time this desire lies at the origin of every variety of animation.[9]

The animation that is the Pokémon is not the object of desire but the object produced by desire and onto which desire can be projected. This is true not only of *Pokémon GO* but had already been the case with *Pokémon Blue and Red* (Game Boy, 1996) which appealed to the gamer in precisely this Lacanian way. Structured by the search for the rarest object, the object that no other Pokémon trainer has, the *Pokémon* series simply simulates the search for the impossible object of desire, with the Pokémon standing in for any other object. What is important is the development between the 20 years that separate *Pokémon Blue and Red* in 1996 from *Pokémon GO* in 2016.

In 2016, the Pokémon is *not* merely displacement or replacement for an already existing object of desire, but the animation of (giving of life to) a desire itself. This is how Freud uses the term "animation" in "The Uncanny" essay, where he employs the earlier English sense of the word, commenting on the "animation of lifeless objects" so that the term describes bringing something to life or "bringing into action" (*OED*)

rather than carrying its later meaning of representation.[10] The Pokémon is born simultaneously
with the desire for it (neither before nor after it is
desired). This can be conceptualized as the difference between 1996 and 2016. Whilst in 1996 the
electronic object was seen as substitutional for the
real one, offering itself as if to an already existing
desire, in 2016 the electronic object gives life to
a new desire entirely. To live in the world of
electronic objects therefore means not to accept
copies and simulations in place of real objects,
as has often been thought, but something quite
different. It means to desire as instructed by the
computer screen, on which the object simultaneously appears and sets desire on its course. In this
way, our computers are oddly perverted in the
fully psychoanalytic sense, forcing their excessive
desires onto us and commanding us to desire via
the assumption that they are giving us what we
want. We can even add that in this regard computers seem to be highly successful perverts.

Depictions of the dystopian videogame future
have always anticipated each individual isolated
from the rest, sat quietly alone in a small room,
and hooked up into a computer through which
their lives are exclusively lived. In other words,

we expected the importance of the physical environment to recede in favor of the imaginary electronic world, but *Pokémon GO* shows that such predictions were wrong. On the contrary to these predictions of the future, we now live in a dystopia where Google and its subsidiaries send us madly around the city in directions of its choosing in search of the objects of desire, whether that be a lover on Tinder, a bowl of authentic Japanese ramen, or that elusive Clefairy or Pikachu. Second, it shows the possibility for the electronic object to replace the real one. The objectivity possessed by the Pokémon is comparable, in a certain sense, to the objectivity of any other "physical" object of desire. Whilst the Pokémon may not have the physicality of a lover who can be accessed via Tindr or a burger that can be located via JustEat, the burger and the lover certainly have the electronic objectivity of the Pokémon. The most important book on electronic objectivity may be Yuk Hui's *On the Existence of Digital Objects,* which showed that while we are often fully aware that digital objects are not concretely present, our relationship to them has still "inherited certain metaphysical presuppositions" so that they are to a certain extent experienced as physical.[11] Yet the focus here is not on how assumptions about objectivity dictate our relations to the electronic object but on how our relationships with electronic objects dictate our consumption of "real" ones.

The relationship between food and Instagram, a recent topic in the study of digital food cultures, proves this point. Whilst Instagram ostensibly celebrates or showcases tasty food, it also obviously plays a role in the transformation of how the foods repeatedly represented actually taste. Common chatter often reminds us that taste is 70 percent determined by smell. And, as Freud knew, the olfactory – far from being natural – is the most ideological of the senses. The repetitious images on Instagram, then, gradually give the food displayed an electronic objectivity one image at a time, transforming the object by endless repetitions which eventually have a concrete effect on the actual taste of the ingredient. Desire for the object, the experience of acquiring it, and the ability to re-share your own consumption of the image, have all been transformed by these technological cycles of repetition. The meal has become Pokémon-like, and, as Srećko Horvat has shown, much the same can be said of the lover whose taste is also transformed by its electronic objectivity.[12] To reverse Groucho's quote (itself famous in its digital existence but possibly never said), you can now only get a decent meal, or a decent fuck, in the virtual world, even when there is a 'real' object in front of you.

From one perspective, the division between Pokémon, dinner, and lovers is erased. It is this power that is important when it comes to the technological trends found in the mobile phone today. To say that these games are revolutionary is of course not to say that they are doing any good, nor that they are "radical," and certainly it is not to say that they are left-wing. On the contrary, the revolution in desire, the "desirevolution," appears to be corporate, hegemonic, and centralized.[13] If attempts at subversion are to have any hope, however, they must not resist *Pokémon GO*, as Sam Kriss of *Jacobin* magazine suggested, but understand and perhaps even embrace the power of the mobile phone to re-organize desire and look for ways forward from there.[14] The term "subversion" has been used in this text with this implication, not to mean resisting technological or social advances but, rather, to mean getting inside such developments and working sub-

24

versively within them. Those dissatistifed with the current political and cultural situation can nostalgically lament that in 2017 even our deepest desires are algorithmic and that a computer knows what we want before we do, or they can be subversive enough to embrace algorithmic thought and learn to think like an algorithm in politically useful ways. Technophilia can be what Nabokov would call "nostalgia in reverse," but a subversive use of technology would eradicate such nostalgia.

As such, *Pokémon GO* introduces the three main arguments of what follows. First, it shows that psychoanalytic concepts of desire, as well as related ideas of condensation and displacement, can allow us to see the function of these games in a new light, revealing how they work not to give us what we want but to transform what and how we desire. Second, it shows that there is a corporate hegemonic control of cyberspace and the world of incessantly changing electronic objects. Third, the desire for the Pokémon can at least potentially confront us with a subversive realization: the realization that the physical object and the desire for it does not pre-exist the mediation of desire via technology. With this made visible, Google cannot claim to simply be giving the user what they want and is revealed instead to be a force that changes our relationship not only to Pokémon but to food, drinks, and lovers, transforming subjectivity. Berardi has called the summer of 2016 the summer of *Pokémon GO*, pointing to the game's function as a distraction from global crises.[15] Yet to be the Pokémon generation means even more than this. It is to be the generation of electronic objects and even of electronic desires. If it can also be the generation that recognizes this, it can break from a long history of ideology and be a generation of great potential subversion.

Level 1

From Farming Simulation to Dystopic Wasteland

Gaming and Capitalism

> It was the dawn of a new era, one where most of the human race now spent all of their free time inside a videogame.
>
> Ernest Cline, *Ready Player One* (2012)

Before getting into the dream analysis of videogames and the potential for subversion found in such experiences, this chapter focuses on the way in which the videogame world is dominated by patterns that endorse protectivism, encourage a fear of "crisis," foster a belief in a particular brand of American progress, and support economic and gendered social norms. In particular this section discusses the ways in which "gaming" can function as a supplement to capital, a kind of ally of the workplace structure and of new state and corporate methodologies of control designed to regulate a restive population. Furthermore, these patterns are found not only in games themselves but in relationships to gaming in a broader sense; in how, where, and why these forms of entertainment are experienced. As such, they go far beyond the world of avid gamers and reflect wider habitual patterns in relationships to consoles, phones, and computers. Perhaps most important is the relationship between games and the workplace and so this chapter focuses on mobile phone and browser games, games that can be played with an Excel spreadsheet open at the same time, to explore the connection between work and play in 2017.

Work and Play

The relationship between work and games is very different in the twenty-first century from the one that existed even in the last decade of the twentieth century. Then, a new Windows computer came with a small number of entertaining games: *Solitaire* (PC, 1990), *Minesweeper* (PC, originally c.1960), or the standout of the bunch, *SkiFree*

(PC, 1991). A computer could connect to the internet, but only via a dial-up connection that could handle loading just one page at a time and made an entire household unreachable by phone. In short, if the user were on the internet, it was the only thing they were doing. The first browser to have tabs, NetCaptor, was developed in 1997, but the need for them was inconceivable to most users at that point and tabbed browsing didn't catch on until over a decade later. Today the average browser has no less than ten tabs running at once, some of which are work and some of which are designated under the heading of "play." The internet functions no longer as an activity but as a background radiation to all of our other actions. In E. M. Forster's 1909 "The Machine Stops," the machine, itself a kind of proto-internet, makes a continuous "hum" that "penetrates our blood, and may even guide our thoughts." This humming noise is imperceptible to those who live with the machine and can only be detected by those who are new to it.[1] The internet is exactly such a machine today, except for the fact that there is no one left to make this observation.

There may be some continuity between old

games and new ones: *Minesweeper*, a forerunner to *Angry Birds* (iOS, 2009); *SkiFree*, a precursor to *Flappy Bird* (iOS and Android, 2013), or *Temple Run* (iOS, 2011). In truth, though, a significant shift has occurred in the relationship between workers and their games. While a few people probably did sneak in some *Solitaire* at work while their bosses' eyes were turned in the late 1990s, these games were primarily enjoyed away from the workplace. The appeal of such games was their ability to sustain players' concentration for several hours at once rather than because of their ability to offer a millisecond of pleasure at every gap in the working day. Thus, *Minesweeper* is more like *Sudoku*, and *SkiFree* is more akin to extreme sports games found in console gaming, perhaps something like *Trials Fusion* (PS4 and Xbox One, 2014). These games require something closer to full attention and in some cases even some critical-thinking skills. Most importantly, they are typically enjoyed during "leisure time" rather than in or around the workplace. By contrast, today's internet tab entertainment and mobile-phone games are designed to be a perfect supplement to the workplace. It is no surprise that statistically the most popular time to play games like *Clash of Clans* (iOS and Android, 2012) is on the commute to and from work and during our lunch hour.

This means that we are in a bizarre second wave of what the Victorians called "rational recreation."[2] That project emerged after 1832, when Britain was as close to political upheaval as it has ever come in modern history – "within an ace of a revolution," according to E. P. Thompson.[3] Through such useful and instructive "rational" amusements as parks, museums, and the promotion of team sports and social clubs designed to group people together in easily manageable clusters, those in power hoped to contain and control a restive population by organizing their enjoyment. Ostensibly, rationality seems to demand the complete opposite today: mobile-phone games and internet tabs encourage individual enjoyment and appear totally useless and uninstructive. Yet while the enjoyments themselves may be different, another wave of controlled recreation today attempts to organize people through their enjoyment, making us work harder for capitalism.

Some games do this by simulating or replacing "success" in the workplace. In a very successful but not at all subversive book on gaming Jane McGonigal argues that *World of Warcraft* (PC, 2004) is precisely such an experience. "What accounts for *World of Warcraft's* unprecedented success?" writes McGonigal. "More than anything else, it's the feeling of 'blissful productivity' that the game provokes."[4] In desperately trying to save her beloved games from those who claim that gaming rots the brain, McGonigal makes a criminal mistake, seeing the capitalist productivity simulated in gaming as inherently positive.

> We've learned that gameplay is the direct emotional opposite of depression: its an invigorating rush of activity combined with an optimistic sense of our own productivity. That's why games can put us in a positive mood when everything else fails – when we're angry, when we're bored, when we're anxious, when we're lonely, when we're hopeless, or when we're aimless.[5]

Here is a dangerously uncritical belief that games are good, that, as McGonigal says, "life is hard, and games make it better."[6] One obvious problem is that if games are experienced as a feeling of productivity, then they have a power to subscribe to us what productivity is. The clearest example would be a game like *Virtual Beggar* (Android, 2016), which tasks the gamer with turning a homeless man into a corporate big cheese, ensuring that gaining capital is associated with success, and with feeling good. This would be an important point even for those giving neurological explanations for the pleasure found in gaming. If such games use imaging and sound techniques to stimulate the neurons, they accompany these technologies with a narrative of capitalist production, establishing an unconscious association between feeling good and a certain formulation of capitalist "success."

Yet there is an even bigger issue here. If McGonigal is right that games can seize us and affect us when we are feeling aimless, hopeless, or anxious – dealing with those feelings of fragmentation and transforming them into something concrete and apparently positive – then this should make the alarm bells ring and cause us to be very suspicious. It shows us nothing more than the extent to which games are powerful ideological tools. Like a nationalist rally in Europe today, they can work on those subjects and in those moments where we feel lost and which seem devoid of meaning. We need only apply McGonigal's suggestion to a first-person shooter like *Medal of Honor: Warfighter* (PC, PS3, and Xbox360, 2012), which aims at "authentically" rendering America's war on terror an experience that the gamer can share in by spraying bullets at Arabs, or *Battlefield 3* (PC, PS3, and Xbox360, 2011), dubbed the "Iraq invasion game," to see the serious problem with the argument. If games can turn feelings of boredom, fragmentation, and depression into productive positivity then we should be careful what ideological structures are being associated with this positive force. In other words, this is not what is good about gaming but what we must be most wary of. We can perhaps say that gaming *interpellates*, the neologism coined by Louis Althusser to describe a process by which the individual is called into a particular subject position. In interpellation, the subject is forced to respond to a prompt in a way that constitutes their subjectivity as the responder in the process. If gaming interpellates fragmented subjects, giving them a sense of purpose, then it does so in the service of dominant ideologies. If gaming appeals to those lost and dissatisfied, as the cliché would have it, it can function to send those people back to "work" by interpellating them into useful ideological subject positions.

Cultures of Distraction

Other games function in a seemingly opposite way, fragmenting the concentration of the worker. Living in what Walter Benjamin had predicted would be a "culture of distraction," we now experience and enjoy hundreds of apparently mindless things that fill our time – not only mobile-phone games and internet tabs but also social-media notifications and YouTube clips. The most popular time to play mobile-phone games, check social media, and visit "listicles" such as Buzzfeed is on the way to and from work or actually from our work computers. The most popular time to tweet is between 11 a.m. and 1 p.m., after two hours at work has begun to breed dissatisfaction and the need for distraction. The most popular time to post a link on Reddit is during work hours on Mondays and Tuesdays, with the week stretching out ahead of us. These distractions, far from being as useless as they pretend to be, are productive and powerful tools that transform us into suitable workers. They set into motion a strange guilt function that turns us into good capitalists and ultimately makes more money for the companies who employ us. In order to have this effect, it is essential that such games are experienced as a complete waste of time. Their purpose is in part to erase a clear distinction between work and leisure so that the worker must "pay back" their *Candy Crush* indulgence by answering emails in bed at night, for example.

Such games aid capitalism not by simulating capitalist success or endorsing its principles, but by appearing to be totally useless and nothing more than a complete waste of precious time. By appearing as such they are able to make the mundane work we perform for capitalism seem so much the more "productive" and "useful" by contrast. After we have "wasted" five minutes on *Cookie Clicker,* we feel like we are carrying out an act that is both productive and reparative when we return to Microsoft Excel afterward. Recent studies have shown that productivity on CRM (Microsoft's data-management server) could be massively increased when workers are allowed to play games for several minutes during the working day and even that videogames have a positive effect on young people's performance at school.[7] Likewise, the company Snowfly specializes in improving company productivity by employing regulated game use in the workplace. In short, we input data quicker after playing a quick round of *Candy Crush*. This demonstrates that these distractions not only consolidate our impression that capitalist productivity is comparatively useful and positive, but also make us feel indebted and keen to make amends to an employer after gaming. Such games are a kind of licensed transgression that not only allows society to continue unharmed, but actually reinforces our desire to pay back what we owe for our little acts of perceived nonconformism. Additionally, they renew our commitment to capitalist production when we might otherwise be reflecting on how unfulfilling our working conditions are.

As such, this investment in cycles of distraction and compensatory productivity can preclude the sort of social interaction that fosters worker solidarity. Consider, for instance, a common scenario just a decade ago, when workers in a hot and physically demanding work environment take hourly five-minute breaks. These five minutes are spent talking with workmates and colleagues. The main subject of discussion is, of course, the only thing the workers all have in common: work. More specifically, the time is used to discuss working conditions, even if that discussion takes the form of rants or simple complaints about long hours, shift patterns, and managers, rather than any organized assessment of the worker in the wider capitalist structure. Now, smokers or not, we take our breaks alone so that we can try to set a new high score on *Smashy Road.* For Benjamin, distraction became an alternative to contemplation, and in the context of the modern workplace we can say that, as such, distracting games are designed to prevent a specific kind of contemplation, that of our working conditions.

This is very much the counterpart of the argument made in the introduction above, and it serves not only the existing structure of work ethic but the increasingly corporate organization of cyberspace. Walter Benjamin's less well-known colleague at the *Frankfurter Zeitung,* Siegfried Kracauer, wrote an essay on Berlin's picture palaces in 1926, with the title "Cult of Distraction." In this short piece, Kracauer seems to anticipate with alarming accuracy the developments of the

Google age. He writes that distraction has been raised to the level of culture and that the result is the creation of a "*homogeneous cosmopolitan audience* in which everyone has the same responses, from the bank director to the sales clerk, from the diva to the stenographer."[8] Like Benjamin, Kracauer wants to reverse the idea that distraction is necessarily the evil and contemplation the good. In our context the opposite of distraction is work, and it is contemplation (of work) which is pressed out. In other words, we can say that the opposite of distraction has become work, with both functioning together in the service of productivity. Whilst concentration has two meanings according to the *OED*, connoting sustained application (working hard) but also reflective consideration (scrutiny of conditions), only sustained application has been retained.

The usual line would be that a culture of distraction prevents us from concentrating on what is really important and doing truly worthwhile things. This often is nothing more than the age-old generational complaint that young people ought to do something better with their time and, worse, it endorses specific ideas of what "worthwhile" time expenditure consists of, just as *Candy Crush* does in the very act of distracting us. The more radical realization is that a culture of distraction doesn't stop us doing really important things; it makes us believe that there actually is something that is really important: capitalist production. Such distractions may appear unproductive but they only serve to focus our faith in that myth.

Pastoral Dystopia, Apocalyptic Utopia

Other games function in yet another way, offering us neither momentary distraction nor capitalist replication but sustained escapism from our own reality. From famous examples such as *The Walking Dead* (PS4, 2012) to *Fallout* (PS3, 1997–present), the gaming industry is currently obsessed with apocalypse. Long a staple of TV and cinema screens, the zombie has now become even more prominent on PlayStations and computers. Added to zombie games are reams of other dystopias, from indie games like *Everybody's Gone to the Rapture* (PS4, 2015) and the cult classic *Soma* (PS4, 2015), to big-budget productions like the *BioShock* series (PS3, 2007–present). As critics like Frederic Jameson, Slavoj Žižek, and Mark

Fisher have all variously pointed out, such images of dystopian futures promote the dangerous idea that only capitalism separates us from a barren wasteland.

On the other side of the gaming spectrum we are offered the opposite: a return to the pastoral past. A useful example is *Stardew Valley* (PC, 2016), an indie-produced farming simulator, or "country-life simulator," which overtook high-profile titles such as *Grand Theft Auto 5* on its release. It might be easier to imagine the end of the world than the end of capitalism, but easier still, it seems, is imagining the resumption of pastoral serenity.

At first glance, one might see *Stardew Valley* as a reincarnation of Zynga's *FarmVille*, the Facebook sensation of 2010. That game offered the chance to nostalgically harvest crops from our computers, but as in other games made by Zynga, such as *Words with Friends* and *Mafia Wars*, the real product being harvested is that of our Facebook friends, whom we put to use to increase our in-game scores (and then turn to for approval for those scores). These so-called social games showed us a very dystopian present in which (as Heidegger suggested) people themselves are as much our raw materials as crops are. But *Stardew Valley* is more complex and has more in common with *Harvest Moon* (SNES, 1996). Like its forerunner Stardew Valley is individual, practically impossible to share or even discuss with friends, and has no multiplayer feature. Far from connecting us to social and technological media, it's an offer to escape from the modern computer society – one we can indulge by sitting in front of our computer screen.

Though they seem to have little in common with gaming's apocalyptic portraits of the future, *Stardew Valley* and other bucolic farming simulators actually provide a necessary counterpart. The gameplay in farming simulators involves organizing people, animals, and the natural environment, planting crops in systematic patterns and experiencing a routine life while playing a key role in a small community. Their picture of a lost era of tightly knit villages where humans lived in organic harmony with nature complements prophesies of a dystopic future in which humans are regimented components of a remorseless capitalistic machine. Farming simulators placate a need for a collective and organized past as an alternative to contemporary chaos, showing the insular and protectivist edge in such experiences of gaming.

This may make *Stardew Valley* seem like a criticism of modern capitalism, but in fact it does little to critique the supposed inevitability of capitalism. Instead it provides the missing piece in a linear account of human history that traces our decline from pastoral paradise to the sterile postcapitalist desert. The best we can do – or so the game tells us - is take comfort in memories and in the fact that we are not further along the inescapable path of destruction. Such games take great pains not to offer an alternative to modern capitalism. As the game's Joja Corporation – a blend of Walmart, Coca-Cola, and Google – starts its inevitable takeover of your peaceful village economy, *Stardew Valley*'s nationalistic indictment of internationalism becomes unmistakable. This is not a subversive critique of corporate globalization but a call for isolationist retreat. *Stardew Valley*'s image of small-scale self-sufficiency draws from the same impulse to erect walls at borders and seek local salvation through exporting immiseration. Tellingly, the village in *Stardew Valley* has a bus stop but the bus has broken down, severing the connection between it and the rest of the world. A real-life example of an alternative to this might be the Catalan communes developing in Spain today, which return to localized production but also use the internet and electronic current to trade across large distances. Such a hybrid of seizing the means of production whilst embracing global technology might assist us in the present crisis, but dreams of being cut off from the internet and the international community do nothing of the sort.

Stardew Valley offers only the consolations of nostalgia, described by Svetlana Boym in *The Future of Nostalgia* as "the search for collective memory, a longing for continuity in a fragmented world."[9] In the past of *Stardew Valley* the gamer can escape to a world where they are "free" to be "human." The game's 16-bit pixelated graphics doubles up this nostalgia, evoking a lost age from the more recent past as well, when video games themselves weren't as complicit and prefigurative of our coming doom – at least in people's memory of them. It incorporates elements of *Zelda, Pokémon,* and other 1990s games that are evocative of a gentler past when games, it is assumed, were more "pure," "organic," and uncorrupted. It was a time when games really

44

were seen as an escape from the political and social world – an argument that seems defunct today, when games seem to more overtly reflect or distill sociopolitical conflicts.

This ambience of escape sets *Stardew Valley* in contrast with *FarmVille*. Whereas *FarmVille* was fully symbiotic with Facebook, seizing on Facebook's technological affordances to propagate itself even as it seemed to soften the social network's neoliberal edges, *Stardew Valley* is more ambivalent about its medium. Its opening scene, a 16-bit reworking of the start of Chaplin's *Modern Times* (1936), presents a bird's-eye view of a regimented contemporary office space, a cubicle farm in which workers are conjoined to computers that are presumably in the process of supplanting them. Trapped in gray walls beneath remorseless fluorescent lighting, these workers are cut off from nature and "real" life, but the game offers us a way out via a faux old-timey letter (obviously not an email) inviting us to return to more authentic work tilling the soil. Of course, this pastoral escape itself demands immersion in a computer simulation. *Stardew Valley* addresses this apparent conundrum differently from *FarmVille*. While *FarmVille* is

45

nothing more than a masked version of social-capital building, *Stardew Valley* seems to want to ironize and distance itself from its simulator nature, using retro qualities as an alibi to make it seem something other than an increased contemporary extension of computerization deeper into our lives.

In presenting itself as a kind of meta-game, *Stardew Valley* confronts players with the bizarre paradox that a return to the past is at once imaginable and impossible. Ultimately, the game's demonstrative awareness of its paradoxical position instantiates Octave Mannoni's idea of Freudian fetishist disavowal: "I know very well, but even so ..." *Stardew Valley* knows very well that it is impossible, but asks us to dream of pastoral serenity anyway. In a strange way this makes the game far more dangerous than *FarmVille.* In *Infinite Distraction* Dominic Pettman writes that contemporary society faces a more sophisticated form of propaganda than that faced in the twentieth century. Now, for example, "new coverage of the race riots distracts from the potential reality and repercussions of the race riots."[10] *Stardew Valley* is just such a form of sophisticated propaganda, ostensibly criticizing capitalism in order to obscure and muffle the possibility of actually critiquing capitalism.

While Mark Fisher might be right when he recently pointed out that dismissing things as "nostalgic" can be a pretty useless gesture, what is needed is further analysis of the peculiar kinds of nostalgia specific to our particular moment.[11] In the case of *Stardew Valley*, its romanticization of the past serves only to solidify our fear of the future. It teaches us to deal with contemporary alienation through wistful backward glances at an irretrievable past. Though it seems innocuous enough, it resonates with Donald Trump's calls to "make America great again," as well as with various European dreams of exiting the EU to return to some prelapsarian national serenity in isolation. Thus, politics play out inside the video-game world. In the years surrounding the Greek referendum, Brexit, and the refugee crisis, when discussions of independent nations have become prominent once again, a stream of nostalgic videogames celebrating national serenity has appeared. Likewise, seven years ago, the financial collapse provoked a ream of dystopian games about capitalism's implosion and pushed the idea that the end of capitalism would essentially mean

endless barren wasteland and/or zombie apocalypse. With online distribution systems and the
mobile game market, videogames can be available only months after they are first hatched as
an idea. This places videogames in a unique position: they can reveal to us the dreams and fears
that we do not yet know we have. *Stardew Valley*
gives this kind of clue for reading the future of its
own moment. It could even be said that all nostalgia contains a potential glimpse of the future
– looking forward rather than back – since it
inaugurates a new relationship to the past that
is heralded and brought into reality by nostalgia
itself.

Stardew Valley's popularity reflects the difficult political position of the potential subversive
today. The fact that internationalism is understood as synonymous with the iniquitous
capitalist disaster of globalization is preventing
the development of solutions on a broad enough
scale to address global crises. This may account
for the return to localism and for the prevalence
of dystopia in popular culture. Writing about
the *Fallout*[12] series, Jeffrey Tam has written that
"dystopian disasters are really just a fresh chance,
an opportunity to simplify our existence and

leave everything behind." The problem we are faced with is not a lack of utopia, because this is really what dystopic dreams are: the enjoyment of a chance to re-start in a more simplified world thinly veiled by the apparent horror of dystopic collapse. In other words, it is utopia repackaged, a kind of Hobbesian "state of nature" that is little more than a projection of what the politics of the present imagine "human nature" would look like.[13] The problem is not that only a ream of dystopias is on offer with no utopian alternatives. It is rather that both dystopia *and* utopia have been appropriated to make capitalism appear to be the "only alternative" by naturalizing a time-line that runs from barbarity to capital. Such patterns aim at the unconscious ingraining of a kind of capitalist conception of history, produc-ing an appearance of uninterruptable linearity from pastoral national serenity to dystopic waste-land. The chance to envisage changes to capitalist modernity is eradicated, leaving only dreams of tempering its destructiveness (*Stardew Valley*) or of starting afresh after the apocalypse (*Fallout*).

No Alternative

So, can games envisage alternatives? One option would be to follow Tam's argument that each dystopian apocalypse is precisely this: an imagined "better future" strangely hidden under the façade of dystopia. In such a reading, utopia is alive and well. Another option would be to run the now well-trodden argument that every attempt to imagine an alternative is yet another symptom of the present and that the dream of a place outside of capitalist modernity would be inevitably nothing more than yet another symptom. The problem is that the possibility of change is hard to accept without a concrete image of what the future would look like. If the adage that it is easier to imagine the end of the world than the end of capitalism has any truth in it, then videogames can save us from this impasse that prevents us from dreaming of alternatives. They can do this not by reviving utopian dreams but by making us see dreams quite differently: as always the symptom of the system from which they emerge. Through this, videogames force us to see that the only future worth asking for is the one not yet concretely imaginable. More importantly, they glimpse a future that already exists, whether they mean to or not.

The inability to imagine genuine alternatives plays out in a whole host of games, including the most apparently innocent. In the 2016 remake of *Ratchet and Clank* (PS4, originally PS2, 2002), a game ostensibly for children, this impasse is embodied: the gamer is presented with a range of right-wing, liberal, or at best pseudo-left options, which give the appearance of genuine choice. This game provides a perfect illustration, but the same logic can be found in many games from this late 1990s/early 2000s era, including the famous *Spyro the Dragon* (PS, 1998) and *Crash Bandicoot* (PS, 1996). Such narratives could be conceived of as evidence of the continuing and far-reaching function of what Mark Fisher called "capitalist realism," the naturalization of a fixed set of possibilities within the system and the smoothing over ("dreamwork") of all potential ruptures so that everything imaginable is subsumed within capitalism. Yet *Ratchet and Clank* accidentally throws us a more subversive realization than Fisher's argument, showing that the future is predicted by the same dreams that are trapped in the present. Such dreams, then, have an immense power that makes them far from futile.

The game's plot reflects an anti-fascist and anti-communist agenda (as if they were comparable), and reflects how Americans perceived ongoing Chinese technological advances as a looming threat to the geopolitical balance in 2002. The evil Chairman Drek, a loosely veiled caricature of a Chinese dictator, plans to build a super-planet he has designed as a "homeland" for his flock of conformist followers. The game begins with a naturally harmonious status quo in which a number of planets flourish independently of each other and with little connection between one planet and the next. Other planets are only accessible through travelling by "galactic spacecraft," even though technology and public transport are both very advanced within some of these planets, showing that what prevents internationalism is politics and not a lack of technology. The early planets in the game are greener and more pastoral, while the later planets (the more evil and difficult ones) are technologically advanced; dystopian metropolises full of threatening warfare and evil technology.

The game therefore associates fascism with acceleration, internationalism, and technology, with its capacity to develop destructive weaponry, complex surveillance structures, secure fortresses, and increasingly regulated conformist societies. Whilst there are indeed fascist accelerationists, here this is used merely as an alibi to present internationalism itself as the fascist eradication of multicultural liberalism. This casts our heroes as stuck in nostalgic backwardness; their values are firmly grounded in the nostalgic past and their quest is to restore pastoral serenity and avoid the evil merging of all the planets into a monoculture. They seek to reinstate the closed borders of each planet and restore everything to its natural and nationalist place. Intended since the Enlightenment to be a universalist philosophy of liberation for everyone, multiculturalism has become a force that sets up essentialist differences between individuals, often of different nationalities, so that the cross-border solidarity that we need more than ever becomes increasingly difficult to foster. This contradiction embodies the crisis in our contemporary political situation, in which people are faced with two ideological options. They can either endorse an international global government run in corporate interests, an option represented by the dystopian vision of Drek and his Blargs, or they can push for a return to the serene nation-state couched in anti-internationalism and nostalgia, represented by Ratchet and the Galactic Rangers, hell-bent on policing any possibility of internationalism. Of course, both options are far from subversive.

This kind of accidental ideology underlying the logic of "the good guys" is a prominent feature of gaming. Like *Stardew Valley* discussed above, *Bastion* (PS4, 2011), for example, is a game with nostalgia at its core. The game takes place in a community that lived in serene harmony until it was infiltrated by monstrous enemies from outside. Our task is to violently rid the community of this external contamination so that it can resume a serene national existence within closed and secure borders.[14] In gaming, our political futures are glimpsed and the rise of the isolationism, nostalgic nationalism, and populism is presaged. This may be because of what former LucasArts director Clint Hocking called "ludonarrative dissonance," a conflict between the narrative and the gameplay. In many cases the game's narrative is an "innocent" or a liberal celebration of generalized humanist values, whilst the structure of the gameplay remains fascist. Espen Aarseth, perhaps the dominant figure in official "Game Studies," has stressed that games are primarily concerned with spatiality and the negotiation of what can be called "ludic" space.[15] Using this model we can say that whilst the narrative overlaying a game may be liberal and humanitarian, the negotiation of space in the gameplay involves the erecting of borders and the expulsion of the other. Such moments threaten to reveal a structural fascism inherent to the narratives of liberalism and humanism, unsettling a distinction between the good guys and the bad guys, precisely what videogames are expected to uphold.

This shows the odd anticipation in early 2016 games of the late 2016 events of the US presidential election and its political confusions. The kind of heavy-handed nostalgia for a bygone (and imaginary) age of national serenity echoes the Trumpian approach which eventually gave him the White House, but this is presented as the characteristic of the "good guys" in the game. Indeed, half of Drek consists of the characteristics of Trump and the other half of Clinton, with the overall sense that capitalist realism has smoothed over the differences between the options so far that the choice hardly matters, even though each are presented in total opposition to one another.

As Yanis Varoufakis has recently written:

> Clinton and Trump are the two sides of the same effaced coin, redolent of the fading illusions of global capitalism's neoliberal turn. The virulent clash between them, just like the clash between David Cameron and Boris Johnson in the Brexit campaign, is masking the fact that the establishment's pro-globalization camp (Clinton and Cameron) and the populist anti-establishment camp (Trump and Johnson) are, in truth, accomplices.[16]

This is exactly the problem facing attempts at constructive subversion or the imagining of alternatives today: they must find a coherent response to the dangerous developments in global politics and technology while avoiding a yearning to be cocooned in the nest of "natural" and national serenity. In this way, patterns of desire underpinning social trends can emerge in the dreamworld earlier than they make their presence felt in politics or other forms of media. Perhaps this is because games are more like dreams than they are like books or movies. As such, they can make visible structures of which they are not yet consciously aware. If Jules Michelet was right that "each epoch dreams the one to follow," then perhaps this now happens through videogames, which don't so much offer an alternative for the future as a glimpse of the future that is already, sometimes unconsciously, here.[17]

This confronts the inadequacy of one of the prominent arguments about capitalism circling in the political and philosophical spheres today: the idea that "there is no alternative." This idea originates in the work of Frederic Jameson and was used by Slavoj Žižek to demonstrate the peculiar capacity that capitalism has to sell its discontents back to the consumer as commodities. Expressions of discontent with the system, from those by Nirvana to *The Hunger Games,* are always-already transformed by the smooth logic of capitalism into the perfect commodities, producing millions of dollars for Hollywood and the corporate music industry in the very act of trying to attack these corporations. Games are of course particularly susceptible to this trap. Another implication of the argument, which came to wider prominence with Mark Fisher's *Capitalist Realism: Is There No Alternative?*, is that every vision of an alternative is already coded within a capitalist discourse, so that each dream of "another way" is seen as a symptom of the system to which it responds. Again, videogames are a form of media often caught in this trap.

Yet this is not as much of an impasse as it may appear. For Žižek, a fundamentally anti-capitalist author and activist, it is important for people to realize that in a certain sense there is "no escape" from capitalism. From this perspective, to be anti-capitalist therefore means not to be outside of capitalism or even to try to get *outside* of it, but to oppose the very structure that you are *inside* and yet be honest about your complicity in it. For Žižek, this was an important point to make in a certain political context, not because it proved that any potential subversives are stuck in capitalism and can do nothing about it but precisely because making this realization would increase the possibilities for changing capitalism from *within*. Fisher's book also ends with optimism for the possibility of change, with the claim that in capitalist realism "even glimmers of alternative political and economic possibilities can have a disproportionately great effect" and can make "anything possible again." Yet Fisher's point contributes to the impression that little can be done aside from waiting for miniature ruptures and "glimmers" of "possibility" that could open up a very closed capitalist system which is highly efficient at smoothing over any cracks and ensuring that everything continues as efficiently as usual. It functions much like the circulating idea today that everyone is caught in an impasse that will be near impossible to overcome, which is a view that comes dangerously close to making an excuse for inaction.

The discussion shows how ubiquitous the word "capitalism" has become, and how important it is to make concrete demands for change rather than demand utopian or dystopian alternatives. If capitalism has become synonymous with concepts like modernity or even with the idea of modern life itself, though inevitably it cannot be escaped the need for it to be changed is even more pressing. Contrary to being the ultimate expression of the deadlock of our modern predicament, the idea that "there is no alternative" should be taken as an opportunity. The world of videogames shows yet more powerful evidence of capitalist realism, as this chapter has in some ways shown. Yet the need to face inevitable change – both corporate and subversive – from *within* means it is necessary to concentrate on the transformations of subjectivity that *are* heralded by today's world of electronic entertainment, rather than those that aren't. Such changes show that whether we find it difficult to create projections of an anti-capitalist future or not, those questions are hardly as pressing as the onrushing transformation of subjectivity, a future that is already here.

Level 2

Dreamwork

Cyborgs on the Analyst's Couch

> The Machine hums! Did you know that? Its hum penetrates our blood, and may even guide our thoughts. Who knows!
>
> E. M. Forster,
> *The Machine Stops* (1909)

The videogame is not a text to be read but a dream to be dreamt. Like a dream and unlike books and television, a videogame is experienced actively, as if each player has a role in determining its events and outcomes. Like a dream, the players experience desires, anxieties, passions, and affects, and they make decisions and take actions according to these semi-instinctive and "emotional" responses. Also like a dream, a lot of this apparent agency is illusory and a player can in fact control neither the environment nor the plot. Even a player's own movements seem somehow governed from elsewhere. Unlike in reality but again like in dreams, the player can be transported from one situation to another with no concern for the laws of time and space. As with dreams, the player returns to the real world afterwards, but things are not always as they were before the dream occurred.

Yet a videogame is not so much the dream of the individual playing but, like all our dreams, is the dream of another. A game is the dream of the designers, the writers, and the illustrators, as well as the producers and, perhaps more broadly, is even the dream of the culture into which the game arises. Ian Bogost sees games as a unique form of media caught somewhere between art, literature, cinema, and sport:

> Games are different from other media. Yes, we "play" games like we do sports, and yes, games bear "meaning" as do the fine and plastic arts. But something else is at work in games. Games are devices we operate.[1]

The problem here is that games are also, and probably more significantly, devices that operate us. With games, then, a different kind of analysis is needed than the kind used to discuss literary texts, for example. Whilst literary studies uses "tools" like "character analysis," "plot structure" and "symbolism," such categories would have little or no use when discussing a videogame (if indeed they have any real use when discussing a book). These analytic tools rely heavily on the idea that the text is representative of reality, and that it comments on or presents reality to its reader, which is only very loosely the case in certain kinds of videogames and in most games does not apply at all. In short, there are no characters, symbols, or plots analyzed in what follows. Instead, there are discussions of patterns, images, displacements, and condensations, repressed wishes and projections: everything that can be found in dreams. This could be described as a psychoanalytic reading of computer games but is more properly an exploration of whether the enjoyment found in computer games can be explained by psychoanalysis. As humans become increasingly machinic – it may be necessary to ask – will psychoanalytic models of subjectivity be useful in the same way? The most important introductory point to this section, then, is that it is always the gamer who is on the analyst's couch and subjected to dream analysis, not the characters found in the "text" or the "text" of the game itself. It is the gamer, as a beta cyborg with machinic and algorithmic but apparently personal and instinctual movements, who must be analyzed.

Japanese Dreams, American Texts

It could be tempting to treat a game like a text. It would certainly be easy to do and it might even look useful. This mini-section shows what it would look like to offer such an analysis of a game, and then offers an alternative approach – the approach of dream analysis – in order to show how different the likely results and conclusions would be. To do this it considers two of the most successful and well-known games in turn, first the best-selling American series *Uncharted* and then the best-selling Japanese series *Persona*. Whilst *Uncharted* is subjected to the literary style of review or analysis that it seems to ask for, dissolving the difference between games and texts,

Persona demands to be read via dream analysis, forcing the gamer onto the analyst's couch and allowing us to see what is unique about the experience of videogaming.

Each of the four *Uncharted* (PS3 and PS4, 2007–16) games, which are some of the most famous, best-selling and highest budgeted of all time, works via a plot with three or four layers. First, there is the search for treasure and gold, embodied by the symbol of El Dorado in the initial *Drake's Fortune*, making our protagonist something of an Indiana Jones figure. Second, there is Drake's quest for love with journalist Elena, the ultimate love object throughout the series, and one who is not "conquered" until the end of the third installment. As some Mexican gangsters tell us at the beginning of the first game, the protagonist is after both girl and treasure simultaneously: "The last man alive gets the gold. Oh, and the girl. Of course." So far, this is typical of most action games or movies. The third layer is the plumbing of the hidden recesses of history in an attempt to unravel the unsolved mysteries of the distant past. A fourth potential layer: it would be easy to argue that the game (as well as Drake) is more than a little guilty of what postcolonial studies calls "Orientalism" – the fetishization of the objects of the East and the desire to plunder the "other." Most of these points could be made about a variety of games, films, and books.

At the end (of each game) Drake gets all four. Predictably, getting one leads to the others – and in the final scene of *Drake's Fortune* this is given the perfect symbolic representation when Drake is handed an ancient ring recovered from the depths of the Orient by his conquered lover. The ring symbolizes love, money, the Orient, and history all together. Given to Drake by his girl, it is a representation of their love. Incredibly expensive, it epitomizes the acquisition of wealth. As the former property of Sir Francis Drake, it signifies the discovery of a lost past. Recovered from the depths of the Amazon, it is a colonial treasure. The ring embodies the Freudian concept of "condensation": when multiple dream-thoughts are combined and amalgamated into a single element such as particular symbol. The root of Drake's anxiety and his obsession with the past is spectacularly revealed halfway through the third game in what is the single most important scene of the quadrilogy and acts as a twist in the narrative trajectory. Here it is revealed that Drake is a lost "Dickensian" orphan who has been missing a purpose from a young age. Placed in an orphanage funded by the Sir Francis Drake foundation, he developed an obsession with the historical figure and named himself after his hero. Walking around museums, Nate becomes driven only by this (imaginary) link, which turns him into a life-long monomaniac: always in manic pursuit of a single thing which, he believes, will provide the fulfillment he lacked as a child and eradicate the anxiety he has long suffered (despite his veneer of bravado). The other characters, Sully (the missing father) and Elena (the replacement mother), as well as the money from treasure-hunting, are all acquired as if accidental symptoms of the more important pursuit of Sir Francis's secrets, but are the objects that in reality have long been sought by Drake's unconscious.

On the surface *Drake's Deception,* the game's title, refers to his deception of others (and of us), but it also more subtly or even unconsciously refers to the way his own unconscious has deceived him through processes of displacement and condensation. Drake, then, is a subject in desperate need of psychoanalysis, and someone that warns us to be aware of how our unconscious is structured.

He teaches us two classic psychoanalytic lessons. First, that we do not want what we think we want and, second, that there is no true desire buried in our unconscious (something which we really *do* want which can come to the surface). Instead, there are only complex displacements and condensations governed by politics and social norms. We learn that neither his quest for money (capitalism), nor marriage (family values), nor the figure of the "other" (Orientalism), nor the past (heroism) are "true" desires. Instead all desires are shown to be just as political as these.

In the above, a videogame has been used to prove psychoanalysis correct, or at best to elucidate some of its lessons. Analyzing the psychological structure of a character in this way is familiar from literary studies or film studies, but sheds little light on the experience of the gamer. The game, in such a reading, shows us something about imaginary others, but very little about ourselves. More importantly, it perpetuates the academic tradition of endlessly proving the same points in new contexts, doing little other than showing that psychoanalysis was right about something.

Some more self-reflective games aim instead

to comment on the experience of the gamer. The most famous of such games is *Persona 4 Golden* (PS Vita, 2012), part of the Megami Tensei franchise originally based on the sci-fi novel series *Digital Devil Story* by Aya Nishitani. This popular franchise has spawned live stage productions, anime series, comics, manga, and countless items of merchandise. Whilst most of the series represents some of the more repetitious forms of gaming such as dance rhythm games and battle simulation, *Persona 4* is a fully immersive narrative that explores the relationship between dreams and games. It can be seen as part of the "Hollywood left" of gaming. In fact, this self-reflective quality seems characteristic of Japanese games, certainly when compared to their American counterparts. The electronic novel *Psycho-Pass – Mandatory Happiness* (PS4, PS Vita, 2016), for example, imagines a dystopia in which the state combats crime by monitoring each citizen's "hue." As in Philip K. Dick's *Minority Report,* a "latent criminal" can be detected when their "hue" rating reaches a certain level. However, unlike that famous sci-fi, there is not an essential propensity for crime in certain individuals but instead everyone is a potential criminal. A citizen's "hue" is transformed by everything from moods and stress levels to ingesting alcohol and watching TV, and each individual must ensure that their "hue" never exceeds a certain level. The question is whether videogames have a detrimental or positive effect on "hue," whether they encourage conformism or criminality, making the game a reading of itself. The "mandatory happiness" society recalls Žižekian discussions of the injunction to enjoy, but the game adds that one must enjoy just the right amount and in just the right ways. Videogaming, though, as the third chapter explores, resists being enjoyed in "just the right way."

Such games break a tradition of trying to immerse the player by making them reflect on the process of playing. *Persona 4* is a murder mystery set in a Japanese high school with supernatural elements. The story has eight playable characters, each of whom is "sucked into the television" by an evil force during the night. Inside the television is a foggy and unclear dreamworld, in which each character has to confront the repressed "side" of their identity. Each character faces an alter ego created out of everything they deny or repress in their daily high-school lives.

There are some questionable elements here, such as the fairly vulgar and homophobic presentation of one character's repressed "homosexual side" and the naturalization of a young girl's desire for sexual exhibitionism. Yet the game is insistent that the player is continually aware of the connection between the experience of the characters and their own experience of being sucked into the Playstation dreamworld as they likewise confront their desires inside the videogame. It seems, then, that *Persona 4 Golden* has a theory of gaming of its own – that videogames reveal to us our repressed desires. Though this argument is countered in what follows here, the idea puts us well into the psychoanalysis of gaming and at least demands self-reflexivity on the part of the gamer.

The Dreamworld

There are four features of the classic Freudian dream, summarized well enough by the Freud Museum:

1. Dreams are the fulfillment of a wish.
2. Dreams are the disguised fulfillment of a wish.

3. Dreams are the disguised fulfillment of a repressed wish.
4. Dreams are the disguised fulfillment of a repressed, infantile wish.

Even the first of these statements is already complex. For Freud, a wish is not just something instinctually wanted or something the subject wants to happen, but a desire instigated by a prohibition. In "The Censorship of Dreams," Freud writes that "dreams are things which get rid of psychical stimuli disturbing to sleep, by method of hallucinatory satisfaction."[2] If games have something of this feature, it is not simply a matter of saying that they give us what we want (i.e. fun or entertainment) but of considering what kind of hallucinatory satisfaction they provide in response to what kinds of cultural prohibitions, interruptions, and frustrations.

The second statement makes this point clear. The game is a disguised fulfillment of a wish, meaning that it is not the game that we want but something else. A clichéd Freudian might argue that the plot and gameplay of each game is enjoyable as a disguised fulfillment of more instinctual desire for sex, and many games would of course bear this out.

A clear example would be the *Dead or Alive* series (1996–present), a program which simply displays a ream of young Japanese women only loosely disguised as a fighting simulator. Anita Sarkeesian, a YouTuber well known to most gamers, has consistently explored the incredible number of exploitative representations of women found in almost every significant game at her channel Feminist Frequency, showing that these titillating images are almost always presented as insignificant supplementary material to the main action of the games. All gameplay could be seen as stand-in for this more instinctual desire and the argument could be extended to every game, since the frustration or displacement of sexual impulse seems not far away even from the grind of *Candy Crush*.

However, the third statement above, that dreams are the disguised fulfillment of a *repressed* wish, throws this oversimplified argument out. Heteronormative sexual desire for objectified electronic women is far from being a repressed desire. It is, on the contrary, something most males are more than confortable with confronting. What desires, then, are such enjoyments (of both the images and the gameplay) to be seen as distorted repressed versions of or substitutions for? It is well known that Freud did not "invent" the concept of the unconscious, but his conception of it broke significantly from other ideas. Where other theorists of the unconscious saw it as a space for the underlying drives which propel us, Freud was clear that the unconscious should be seen as by definition unknowable and necessarily resistant to conscious articulation. As such, once a desire is identified and designated, it is no longer or never was in the realm of the unconscious. However, this is not to say that the unconscious should not be interpreted. The fourth and final statement, that dreams are the disguised fulfillment of a repressed, *infantile* wish, needs qualifying in these terms. Infantile need not be thought of as instinctual, with its associations with the natural, but should be thought of instead as a foundational or formative desire. It is *drive* rather than instinct, a distinction made by Jacques Lacan:

> *Trieb* gives you a kick in the arse, my friends – quite different from so-called *instinct*. That's how psycho-analytic teaching is passed on.[3]

Drives move us forward, propelling us *as if* from within, but they do not originate from the inside.

In other words, while our instincts (insofar as they exist) to a certain extent belong to us, our drives certainly do not. Like a decision made inside the virtual dreamworld, we are given a kick in the arse but nevertheless feel instinctive agency driving us in the directions in which we move.

With the implications of the four statements considered, Freud's argument needs to go one step further than he took it. While Freud might argue that dreams are the disguised fulfillment of a repressed, infantile wish, in the context of this discussion the diagnosis can be reformulated in the following way: dreams are disguised *as* the fulfillment of a repressed, infantile wish. Whilst the dream is the dream of the other, it is disguised as the fulfillment of the subject's internal or instinctive desire. Dreams give us a kick in the arse, coming from outside like a drive, but they can appear to be propelled from instinct or internal desire. In fact, though later commentators neglected to notice, when Freud used the term "infantile" to describe "wish" he did not mean instinctual desires. In the case of subject Professor R, for instance, he notes that the realization of one of the "immortal infantile wishes" was "the megalomanic wish," which is instilled by cultural factors.[4] It would be better to conceive of such dreams as carefully constructed ideologies which appear to be internal impulses.

Videogames, then, insofar as they are the experience of another's dream, can be a unique form of enjoyment in which the wishes and desires of another are experienced – perhaps momentarily and unconsciously – as the wishes and desires of the gamer's own. It is this peculiar brand of enjoyment which can be at once the most ideologically dangerous and the most subversive, which makes such experiences central to our conceptions of enjoyment in a wider sense. Thinking first of the purely ideological side of this function, games can naturalize the enjoyment of the other, forcing the player to feel a kind of affinity between themselves and the role they play within the game when they fall into the dreamlike gamer state. This is often not as simple as direct identification with a playable character and is a more complex connection between the unconscious of the gamer and the unconscious of the game. In such moments the player increasingly feels their emotions programmed by the game's algorithms. In this sense desire is becoming increasingly algorithmic and videogames are playing a key role in this reorganization of desire. This is a particular concern considering that increasing corporate organization of technological space means increasing potential for corporate control of desire itself, as discussed above.

This can also be understood in the terms of the unconscious. Of course, games reflect unconscious dreams, wishes, and desires, but they also play a role in constructing these unconscious assumptions. So far, this is nothing so different from other forms of media. Yet games have a particular and more unique role in this construction: the role of naturalizing the dreams, desires, and wishes of a political moment by making us experience those dreams, desires, and wishes as our own. Furthermore, as has been intimated, since the desires and wishes of a political moment can be unconscious to that moment itself, games have a quality of being able to predict as well as construct the dreams of the future.

There are two ways, then, in which this corporate "desirevolution" could be turned on its head via this same dialectical ideological enjoyment that it creates. The patterns of enjoyment found in the videogame dreamworld tend toward the enforcement of traditionalist and conservative values which support the core values of contemporary capitalism or move them further to the political right. This is less because the structure of videogames is inherently conservative or reactionary per se and more because the dreamworld is a reflection and even anticipation of coming political and social trends. Yet, if games serve the function of naturalizing forms of ideological enjoyment, could they not do for a subversive agenda what they appear to have been doing for corporate and state powers? Could we conceive of a videogame which aims at reprogramming desire against the fascist, corporate, and capitalist tendencies found in videogames in general, or would the only "morally ethical" game be the kind which denaturalized desire, showing our wishes to be not natural but the naturalized wishes of the other? This is a question about the politics of subversion in a much wider sense, since embracing this possibility would involve an admission that it is necessary not only to deconstruct existing ideological assumptions but to construct new ones, operating consciously to manipulate the emotions of others. It may be time for the left to accept this necessity.

Yet, even without the potential of a radical subversive revolution in videogaming, the ideological enjoyment found in gaming threatens to turn inside out and subvert the very organization of desire that it simultaneously enacts. Since videogames can naturalize forms of enjoyment in the service of ideological forces, so too do they have the potential to make this naturalization visible, unseating the connection between enjoyment and nature and showing the political structure of enjoyment. The experience of algorithmic desire only works because it is not experienced as wholly algorithmic. On the other hand, making visible the algorithmic structure of desire undoes its ideological function. If videogames can naturalize programmed desires, as explored further below, they can only do this by making the gamer experience such desires as natural. This kind of desire reprogramming can only function on its subjects if those subjects don't realize what is happening and instead remain invested in a traditional idea of desire as free from politics. Even if we "know" that there is nothing instinctive about the desires and enjoyment experienced in the game, it is nonetheless important that such enjoyment is experienced *as if* instinctual. The corporate desirevolution, then, a reorganization in the service of Silicon

Valley, works not only by algorithmically repro-gramming desires but also by hiding this fact so that desire is experienced as an enchanting moment of authentic yearning for the object in question. Recognizing the programmable nature of desire – a psychoanalytic realization – upsets this traditional way of seeing desire which serves corporate interests, so that gaming, in all its conformism, has acquired the potential to undo this logic from within.

Repetitions and the *Dromena*

One of the major appeals of videogames, from the simplest mobile-phone applications to the most complex console games, is that of their repetitious patterns. In certain cases games may function to encourage repetition in the gamer since subjects are easily governable when they stick to repetitious routines like those discussed in the introduction. Yet, in other cases, the repeti-tion serves to ingrain not only the compulsion to repeat itself but particular ideological ideas. The previous chapter outlined some of the ideological and political trends found inside the videogame dreamworld and the repetitious nature of gaming may be a way for these politics to be ingrained, often unconsciously, upon the gamer.

This repetitious function of videogames can be illuminated by an old philosophical idea: the idea of *dromena*. *Dromena* literally means "things which are left running," but it is also to be taken with its onomatopoeic implication: things which drone on and on, repeating again and again in endless cycles. In his recent book on the role of the pleasure principle in contemporary culture, Robert Pfaller gives the example of schoolchildren forced to repeatedly write lines such as "I will not fidget during class" as a punishment for fidgeting. After writing the line a hundred or so times, it is imagined, the idea will stick in a more unconscious way and the child will no longer fidget in class. Likewise, clicking thousands of times in a capitalism-simulation game such as *Virtual Beggar* or *Cookie Clicker* (PC, 2013) may unconsciously encourage you to click more efficiently on your work computer.[5] Similarly, shooting a million bullets in the service of American foreign policy, no matter what your conscious objections may be when you are not in the game, may ingrain the ideology at another more unconscious level, or so the typical argument would go.

Yet Pfaller also makes the more interesting case for the reverse of this argument: that "the repetition of symbols can also cause one to have as little as possible to do with these symbols and the situation they describe."[6] When the symbol has been repeated so many times, the subject is able to repeat it or see it repeated while thinking about something completely different. Slavoj Žižek has written similarly that while going through a process of *dromena,* "the beauty of it is that in my psychological interior I can think about whatever I want."[7] The insight is particularly pertinent for a discussion of videogames, which can also be very clearly seen as a kind of repetitious *dromena,* with cyclical repetitions, level after level, sequel after sequel, which gamers opt to compulsively re-enact. Could this be exactly the way in which videogames appeal? By inviting us into a process of *dromena,* the user can go wherever they want psychologically, and thus games can offer a kind of escapism which goes beyond that offered even by the most involving book or film.

Neither the idea that *dromena* ingrains symbols onto us by repetition nor the alternative that it frees us from the need to think about these symbols seems sufficient. On the contrary, it is in the relationship between these two apparently opposing ideas of *dromena* where a third and more satisfying answer can be found. It is precisely the feeling of freedom which allows us to imagine that in our psychological interiors we can think about whatever we want, that enables ideology to be effectively imposed by the repetitious patterns in the gaming experience. It is because we *feel* free to allow our thoughts to wander while we are gaming that the game's ideology can be imposed on us. Of course, what we "freely" think while our minds drift from the *dromena* of gaming is not as free as it may seem, so that we cannot really "go where we want" psychologically. This is another characteristic shared between videogames and dreams, especially in Walter Benjamin's conception of dreams in which the dreamer's mind wanders as if freely into atmospheres created by politics and ideology.

A fantastic and simple example of this would be the most apparently innocent and apolitical game of all, the award-winning *Flower* (PS3, 2009), as well as its precursor *Flow* (PC, 2006) and successor *Journey* (PS4, 2012). In *Flower*, the user plays as "the wind" and moves through the natural environment collecting beautiful petals in endless *dromena*-like cycles. It looks as though the player is free to let their mind wander, and indeed the game is designed to encourage relaxation and contemplation. Yet, of course, *Flower* is full of ideology, evoking the beauty of the natural world, fetishizing the "uncontaminated" pre-human environment and showing all sorts of resistance to any form of technological advance. The game's developers have spoken of the company's philosophy, saying that they work from the initial premise of considering what kinds of "emotion" they want to evoke in their gamers, showing the ability and even direct intention of games to make the gamer experience the programmed emotion as their own. In the *dromena* of playing, we are free to wander and let our minds drift, but where they drift is somewhere new, a new dream dictated at least in part by the drometic structures of the game we drift away from.[8]

In other words, games make us think, whilst also making us feel that we are free to think as we like. Rather than freeing the mind of the gamer to go where it pleases, this kind of *dromena,* at least, and perhaps all kinds, put you into a dreamlike state from which its ideology is imposed as natural. We can perhaps borrow Louis Althusser's term again and say that the videogame interpellates, calling the subject into a particular subject position but, more than this, insisting at the same time that the subject always-already belonged in this position in order to respond to the call. We could also say that with videogames we really are in the realm of emotions rather than the realm of affect. This would be the opposite of a general and critical trend in videogame discussions, which tends to focus on the affectual quality of such entertainment. Even though both cultural and scientific approaches focus on the neuron-stimulating affectual capacity of the videogame screen, while it may look this way from the outside, most gamers would not describe their enjoyment or investment in gaming as primarily affectual at all. Freud prefers the term *affect* to emotion because whilst the concept of emotion has a humanist quality and implies a feeling that comes from within, *affects* are sensations felt on the boundary between the body and the outside world. In gaming, though, we may need to reinstate the term "emotion" and remember the distinction, since it appears that games function rather to turn affects into emotions, making the gamer experience something from without as if from within.

Immersion and *Westworld*

This points to the importance of immersion, which developments in Virtual Reality over the next few years aim to make complete. Games have never struggled to be immersive, but the development of PlayStation VR, for example, released in October 2016, works significantly to erase the gap between – for example – the character on screen and the gamer on the couch. Yet immersion is less about the completion of perfect realism than it seems. In light of what has been put forward in this book so far, immersion is less about making the experience of gaming appear as close to reality as technologically possible and more about the gamer entering the perfect dream-state in which the game can have the greatest effect. It is not that VR companies are aware of this and consciously seek to achieve this to advance an ideological agenda but that this is the dominant unconscious driving force behind the production of VR. Edwin Montoya Zorrilla has already shown that Chris Milk's company Within, which uses VR film to evoke empathy and encourage charity, may be doing a good deed, but that such tactics reveal more about the dangerous power of VR to make the participants want to do things.[9]

The general fear of immersive VR is grounded in the idea that the virtual world, when it becomes near indistinguishable from the real one, will be more appealing than reality and people will opt to remain in the game, perhaps endlessly. The best summary of the situation is that of André Nusselder, who writes:

> The standard fantasy about new worlds opened up by computer technologies considers them as spaces where all the old limits might be transcended. The offer to relieve us of the burdens of reality. From a Freudian perspective, this wish-fulfilling aspect of technology functions as the realized fantasies of a hallucination.[10]

Yet, as Nusselder goes on to explore, the implication that cyberspace is nothing more than an illusory world of appearances, a false version of what we really want, is inadequate and over-simplifies the distinction between illusion and reality. This is in fact an argument that permeates theoretical and everyday approaches to both videogame studies and psychoanalysis. Both academic and general commentators often remark that games allow or simulate the fulfillment of basic impulses and desires shared by all humans. Psychoanalysis has also been read and used in this way, with desire for instant gratification and the desire for the mother (to take two examples) often taken to be transhistorical "human" fantasies, components of the human condition *as such*. VR, we assume, allows us to realize, albeit in fantasy, these shared universal human drives.

Jonathan Nolan's pop-Freud HBO TV-series *Westworld* (2016) makes this point. The premise of the show, a remake of Michael Crichton's 1972 movie, is that a technological corporation creates a fully immersive virtual-reality world full of robots who are ostensibly indistinguishable from humans. This world is given a Wild West setting and functions more or less straightforwardly as a projection screen for the basic desires apparently shared by all humans. In the Westworld Theme Park, paying guests are free to murder, rape, and sadistically enact any desire they may have on the robots, with no fear of repercussion, yet at the same time are fully immersed in the possible dangers of these acts while in the illusion of the "game."

What is interesting in the show is that desire is shown to be more complex than the corporation assumes and a large number of guests find that they have an odd relationship to what the company considers to be transhistorical desire shared by all humans. A number of characters refuse the logic of the corporation, saying that they do not share these apparently universal human drives with other "players." They argue instead that their own desire is fundamentally more complex and perhaps more refined or historical, not reducible to basic transhistorical models of basic human impulse. Yet things do not get interesting until these very characters who champion the idea of desire as historical and irreducible to basic universal instinct begin to enjoy those things they originally rejected, slipping into the violent and sexual actions encouraged by the game. The typical reading of this would of course be that the TV show endorses the idea that no matter how culturally refined we *think* our desires may be, deep down we are all the same primal beings. Yet *Westworld* heads off this interpretation, showing that the experience of being in the park not so much shows who the players really are but changes who they are and how they desire.

In his popular dystopian novel of 2012, *Ready Player One,* Ernest Cline creates a world in which "most of the human race now spent all of their free time inside a videogame" that transforms "entertainment, social networking and even global politics."[11] He presents two different ways of seeing the "OASIS," which is a hyperbolic internet-videogame space combining massively multiplayer online gaming with social media, in which everyone lives as their avatar. The main character in the novel believes that the experience of the OASIS is liberating because in the OASIS appearances do not matter and "we exist as raw personality in here," just as the corporation sees the Westworld Theme Park. The other central character disagrees, giving the more standard line about social media: "everything about our online personas is filtered ... which allows us to control how we look and sound to others. The OASIS lets you be who you want to be. That's why everyone is so addicted to it."[12] Such positions are both clichés about social media and about videogaming, and both rely on the idea that the dreamworld is a space for the fulfillment of desires without recognizing the power of the space to transform desire itself. *Westworld,* on the other hand, confronts us with exactly this, showing that the principal function of the virtual technological space is not to let us be who we want to be, nor to give us what we want, but to change what and how we desire.

Psychoanalysis teaches that desire is always the desire of the other. This means not just the desire *for* the other (i.e. longing for the attractive robot in the Westworld Theme Park), but the desire that is set in motion by the desire of the other. It is not even enough to say that we want to be wanted, which is an abstraction from psychoanalysis that has become common discourse. Instead, it is that we want to want as the other wants. Desire itself has an imitative quality, so that there is no original desire and certainly no transhistorical impulses. Psychoanalysis, then, makes the opposite argument to the one usually attributed to it, arguing that any shared or comparable desires we may have originate not from instinctive human impulse but from a much stranger attempted imitation. Here, then, shown to us by *Westworld,* is the incredible power of the ideology of transhistorical desire. In constructing an other who desires as such, the image of a transhistorical subject presented (by those with corporate interests) as universal, it becomes possible to set in motion a desire which operates in an imitative relation to this image of a universally desiring human, with all its barbarism and patriarchal sexual instinct. The image of an other who desires in this apparently primal way is enough to create the possibility of the subject desiring as this other desires, not because all subjects have such desires but because desire is imitative.

Such a realization is significant for the theory of videogaming. When parents lock up their children's copies of *Grand Theft Auto* or *Hotline Miami* (PC, 2012) and *Not a Hero* (PS4, 2015), they do not so much keep their kids civilized as help to construct them as subjects full of uncivilized desires. The two positions on the impact of such GTA-style games are: (a) that young people will replicate what they experience in games, causing violence; and (b) that videogames provide a safe outlet for such dangerous drives, preventing violence. In fact a third position, one that doesn't assume the pre-existence of such drives, is needed to see how such games and the assumptions accompanying them function to construct new subjects with new desires. The longstanding idea that videogames appeal to these basic transhistorical configurations of desire produces an imagined "other" who desires as such and invites the gamer to desire on these terms. Thus, videogames do not reflect what we want deep down but construct "others" whose desires we imitate.

So, rather than appealing to universal desires, videogames can program the user to desire in a universal way. At the same time, they can threaten the logic that sees humans as universally desiring organisms. If the gamer realizes that they experience not their "own" desire but the desire of the other, the apparently natural connection between desire and subjectivity is conceptually threatened, showing desire as neither universal nor unique but constructed politically as such. Hence, a particular kind of simulated "empathy" is made possible via videogames. This is not an empathy which assumes understanding of the other and erases difference by implying affinity – an empathy that Jacques Derrida warned against – but a simulation of the other's enjoyment which makes visible both the structure of the other's pleasure and the structure of the subject's own.

Level 3

Retro Gaming

The Politics of Former and Future Pleasures

> We are cyborgs. The cyborg is our
> ontology; it gives us our politics.
> Donna Haraway, *The Cyborg Manifesto*

Lacan's major project was to explore enjoyment
rather than pleasure or desire. For Lacan, enjoyment was the thing for which structuralism and
other existing models of philosophy had most consistently failed to account. Whilst the importance
of enjoyment can hardly be overestimated culturally, socially, and politically, philosophy seems
never to properly grasp its functions. Speaking
of the enjoyment of games, Bogost accounts for
the yield of pleasure derived from gaming by sug-
gesting that in some cases gaming may replicate

94

other "older" forms of enjoyment. He compares, for example, the satisfaction of *Flappy Bird* with the pleasure derived from fixing a bathroom cabinet. This is a position which risks neglecting the revolution in enjoyment that has been heralded by advances in technological entertainment and coming down on the side of consistency in human enjoyment. Despite this, the interpretation gives us a clue as to the way in which much technological entertainment is enjoyed: by apparently recovering lost enjoyment. This makes gaming an important intersection between past and present.

Rational Gaming in the 1990s

Retro gaming is the most obvious form of gaming whose pleasures are found directly in the desire to recapture former enjoyments. Like the appeal of a lover from the past to an ageing singleton, the games of our youth nostalgically appeal to us in strange ways. Speaking of retro technology, Grafton Tanner has argued that whilst modern technology is ubiquitous and smooth, technology in the 1980s and 1990s was incredibly unsettling.[1] Tanner evokes the concept of "the uncanny" to describe the regularly malfunctioning and misperforming machines of yesteryear. A more subversive point would be to say that former technology is only *now* found uncanny and that this uncanniness is evidence of our new cyborg-like subjectivities. For something to be experienced as uncanny in the properly psychoanalytic sense it must have a special relationship to the formation of the subject who experiences the sensation. For Freud, the feeling of the uncanny arises when a foundational process that constructs subjectivity (repressed by the idea that subjectivity is natural) comes to light. As such, if glitches in machinery feel uncanny to us, it is because they remind us of our former machinic subjectivities, of the prototype machinery for something now so smooth-functioning and ubiquitous as to seem to be a natural and inevitable part of our consciousness. In simple terms, the idea is that it is only because we are machines that machines can be uncanny, rather than because the machines are like humans (which is merely "strange").

Yet playing an old game is rarely uncanny. On the contrary, some games seem to lose their uncanniness with time as capitalist realism smooths over their inconsistencies. One example of this is *SkiFree*. After almost 25 years buried in the recycle bin of our unconscious, the 1991 Windows classic experienced a return in 2015, but the experience of playing this subversive game from the early 1990s had fundamentally changed. In 1992, when it was released as part of the Microsoft Entertainment Pack for Windows 3.1, *SkiFree* stood out as totally anachronistic. To give some context, the Microsoft Entertainment Pack was well known for games like *Minesweeper*, *WinRisk*, and *Solitaire*. Each of these required active and challenging mental work on the part of the participant. *Minesweeper* was yesteryear's Sudoku, *WinRisk* was derived from the strategy-board game, and *Solitaire* is a notoriously taxing card game of the same name. Each of these exemplifies the demand for a constructive use of leisure time meant to enrich the mind, cultivate one's critical faculties, and ultimately help the subject to become a useful citizen. Windows 3.1 was a bastion of "useful" and ostensibly "interesting" semi-educational games that ran the gamut from *Chessnet* to *Election '92*, but *SkiFree* was the subversive alternative to these trends.

The premise of *SkiFree* is that the player chases other skiers while crashing into cable cars, murdering animals, leaping over trees, and setting things on fire. There is no goal and no way to beat the game. Instead, the player is eaten by an iconic yeti after several minutes of play, regardless of their actions. The most experimental and experienced players might remember that if the player pushed the game's boundaries, its reality became blurred: certain trees would move and grow feet (if observed carefully) and (if the player skied backwards over certain tree stumps) they could turn into mushrooms. If the player deliberately used their skis to murder a large number of dogs they would start staining the snow yellow. The "glitches" were built into the game as a deliberate part of its logic in order to reveal how smooth-functioning the rest of the computer system was attempting to be. The deliberate "glitch" pointed to the power of the real glitch, which revealed that the components of Windows 3.1, from spreadsheets to games, attempted to cohere toward a particular kind of productivity

SkiFree mocked the idea of useful time expenditure and asked us to dive into a mad waste of time with no end "goal" in sight. As a result, it had a subversive premise in which enjoyment derived from the game was not measurable, no one gained from playing it (neither the user nor their boss), and no personal improvement occurred. It was not capitalist pleasure but troubling *jouissance* (more later). Even Chris Pirih, the game's creator, did not make money from the game. *SkiFree* was the bad egg refusing to "work," undermining everything Windows seemed to stand for, tempting us to click on it and reject Microsoft Office and its accompanying army of productive "games." Some 25 years later in January 2016, when *The Windows 3.x Showcase* was launched, making *SkiFree* available once more, within a week the game had become the most popular item on the site with tens of thousands of plays. *SkiFree*'s reappearance though, within the context of this age of mass distraction discussed in chapter 1, is hard to qualify as subversive. Now it embodies the "useless," "distracting," and apparently "wasteful" enjoyment that has itself become rational and useful, a type of enjoyment that perfectly complements and enhances the agenda of capitalist productivity. Capitalism has got smarter at covering up its cracks.

In this example, lost enjoyment cannot be recovered because the meaning is so dependent on the technological context of the gamer. In fact, retro gaming in the sense of playing an old *Space*

Invaders arcade machine is relatively unpopular and belongs more to the ethos of straightforward nostalgia, but what is highly popular are modern reworkings of old games which now function smoothly, and new games which nostalgically incorporate features of past technologies. Important examples include *Undertale* (PC, 2015) and *To the Moon* (PC, 2001) but the most indicative example is the "visual novel" *Emily Is Away* (PC, 2015). Set in 2002, the game is a simulation of a chat-client conversation that takes place over four years of American high school. The game reincarnates the "dating simulators" popular in the late 1990s. The player flirts with the protagonist Emily, discusses her tempestuous relationship with a long-standing love interest, and eventually loses touch with her as she moves on with her life and ceases to reply. The game is designed to replicate the desires of the past by recovering the lost pleasure of the teenager in the chat room. This is an uncanny experience in both obvious and complex ways. As a return of the millennial teenager to its adult persona, it is the reminder of the repressed former self, both deeply enjoyable and unsettling. More importantly, as an example of the cyborgs of 2017, it is a reminder of the technologies on which subjectivities are based. In this sense the uncanny is a theory of technology.

Since the contemporary situation is such that no form of enjoyment disappears, the world described by Mark Fisher seems truer than ever: "in conditions of digital recall, loss is itself lost."[2] Yet, if in the digital age loss itself takes on the peculiar quality of being lost, then digital nostalgia may work not by rediscovering something lost but by returning loss itself to us. If games show us the pleasure yielded from the return of the subject to loss itself, then they can also operate as a critique of how nostalgia works politically. By showing that nostalgia is not a yearning for specific past politics (national/natural serenity, for example), but an affect of the present which can harness the loss of loss to assert a political agenda, such experiences warn gamers to be critical of political nostalgia.

Virtual/Reality

The same decade that rationalized and organized gaming in the service of work also brought the most philosophical and bizarre games to date, not just as momentary hiccups but as sustained investigations into the emerging relationship between reality and the virtual. In 1993 Nintendo released Takashi Tezuka's masterpiece, the strangest of the Zelda series, *Link's Awakening* (GB). Tezuka and his team worked out-of-hours with no official remit from Nintendo and produced a unique subversive commentary on gaming. Recently, *Electronic Gaming Monthly* called *Link's Awakening* the "best Game Boy game ever, an adventure so engrossing and epic that we can even forgive the whole thing for being one of those 'It's all a dream!' fakeouts."[3] This is a typical neglect of the complexity of gaming narratives, which, since long before the 1990s, have been much more complex than copies of clichéd film narratives. Tezuka's principal inspiration was Lynch's *Twin Peaks* and the game involves a conscious engagement with the effect of emerging technologies of immersive gaming on conceptions of dreams and reality.

The game contains unpredictable cameo appearances from characters who belong within the limits of other videogames. These include Yoshi and Kirby, as well as the lesser-known Dr Wright from *SimCity* (PC, 1989) and characters from the existential Japanese game *The Frog for*

Whom the Bell Tolls (*Isaeru no Tame ni Kane wa Naru*, GB, 1992; still not available in English), whose engine was used to build *Link's Awakening.* This forces the gamer to confront the possibility of crossing between imaginary boundaries, since players were familiar with these other characters and experienced their separate games as a kind of realism with guaranteed limits. The encounter with the alien character shattered this realism. It was not experienced as parody, as it would be in comparable examples of cameo-characters in film, but as an odd reminder that the limits of the gamer's perception are sustained only by the game designers entrusted with keeping them in place.

Such moments are a better definition of the uncanny than the more traditional one given in the previous section. Rather than the "return of the repressed," which validates a spatial metaphor for subjectivity that casts humans as those who "bury" aspects of themselves only to see those elements "resurface" in other forms, the uncanny should be seen as nothing other than the switching of an object from one linguistic register to another. The Lacanian revolution in psychoanalysis insisted that repression has to do with language and involves putting something into a narrative in order to make sense of and control it. Jean-Luc Nancy writes that the unconscious is "not at all another consciousness or a negative consciousness, but merely the world itself," the totality of signifi-ability.[4] It is in this precise sense that cyberspace is a dreamworld, since it connects the user not to their internal unconscious but to the uncon-scious-as-the-world. Banishing something to the unconscious does not mean burying it *deep within* but rather excluding it from the "reality" of a given narrative or moment. When Yoshi appears next to Link, a feeling of the uncanny is produced, just as when dreams about our lover are interrupted by images of our mother. It is not that true desire for the mother has been buried and has accidentally come to light, as traditional readings of Freud held, but that the image of the mother belongs in a different register to the image of the lover, due to the organization of subjectivity via lan-guage. A similar maintenance of distinct linguistic registers maintains the distinction between reality and dreams and between intelligence and artificial intelligence, all of which become uncanny when the boundary of the register is threatened.

In this regard, the real subversive quality of *Link's Awakening* appears via the plot. The story takes place not in Hyrule (the imaginary land in which Zelda games are set), but inside the dream of the "Wind Fish" – a giant sleeping creature. The gamer's quest is to awaken this creature from its lengthy sleep and send everyone back to reality. Link, the gamer imagines, would return to Hyrule, whilst the gamer would return to the "real" world. The twist comes at the midway point of the story, when the characters begin to notice that the gamer is working toward shattering the reality on which their lives and the lives of their families depend. When defeated, the bosses beg for their reality not to be destroyed:

> Why did you come here? If it weren't for you, nothing would have to change! You cannot wake the Wind Fish! Remember, you too are in the dream …

Link is faced with the famous problem that would confront Neo in *The Matrix* some six years later: take the red pill (wake the Wind Fish) and embrace the painful truth of reality, or take the blue pill (leave it asleep) and remain within the blissful ignorance of illusion.

Yet *Link's Awakening* does more than antici-pate the Wachowski Brothers' idea. Whilst the "matrix" depends on those inside being unaware of the illusion in which they live, this is not the case in *Link's Awakening,* where the inhabitants continually make it clear that they know that they are inside the "matrix." As one character says:

> My energy ... gone ... I ... lost! But you will be lost too, if the Wind Fish wakes! Same as me, you are in his dream.

Slavoj Žižek analyzed the choice presented to Neo in *The Matrix,* claiming that neither choice is subversive enough:

> I want a third pill. So what is the third pill? Definitely not some kind of transcendental pill which enables a fake, fast-food religious experi-ence, but a pill that would enable me to perceive not the reality behind the illusion but the reality in illusion itself.[5]

Žižek argues that reality cannot be accessed by bypassing illusions, since reality is always mediated through the stories we tell about it. Yet, whilst this means that illusions are inescapable, there is no reason we need to be ignorant of this situation. In fact, the function of ideology is to insist that we experience our illusions whilst believing them to be reality. *Link's Awakening*, then, gives us the "third pill" that Žižek asks for. The game is not about a choice between living in blind illusion or facing the harsh truth but about recognizing that illusions are necessary for the production of reality. The characters in the game may not want their world destroyed, but this is not the same as opting to remain within the "matrix." Instead, there is an awareness of the truth of illusions, that there is no reality outside of illusion, that "there is nothing beyond the sea," as the game tells us.

Gaming often involves this temporary psychoanalytic disavowal, with the gamer knowing very well that they enter a world of illusion and yet still experiencing the game as reality alongside full awareness of this. The work of Fox Harrell – along with Wark discussed above – is one of few convincing attempts to explore the potentially subversive qualities of gaming. Speaking of online avatars, for instance, Fox Harrell has shown "the impact of virtual identities on real world identities," identifying a performative quality in gaming rather than seeing a phenomenon like the avatar as a simple reflection or projection.[6] This is something discussed much earlier in a groundbreaking essay by Bob Rehack in Judith Butler's *Excitable Speech,* which in 1997 prophetically anticipates many developments in videogaming that occurred after 2010. There, Rehack sees the avatar as involving an odd repetition of Lacan's mirror stage, splitting the subject from the image of itself and provoking endless circles of anxiety and reparation which have a concrete effect on subjectivity.[7] The relationship between reality and the virtual ought to be seen as dialectical, so that games are seen to change our relationships to reality as much as they are informed by or reflective of it. At the same time, they can also be an experience that confronts the gamer with this realization, showing how interdependent reality and the virtual can be. Such a realization makes it apparent that escaping the virtual in favor of reality is an impossibility, stressing the need for subversion *within* technology and *in* the virtual world in place of technophobia.

Subject, Object, Enjoyment

It is argued above that the enjoyment of videogaming is found in the pleasure yielded from experiencing the enjoyment of the other. In most cases, this other's enjoyment is presented as exciting and idealized, hence the general conception that games allow office workers to experience the adrenaline rush of superheroes. However, the pleasure yielded from the experience of the other's enjoyment functions whether or not the other is doing anything exciting. In regard to making this strange pleasure visible, a genuinely subversive corner of the videogame dreamworld is the "dystopian document thriller" *Papers, Please* (2013), an award-winning PC, iOS, and PS Vita game designed by Lucas Pope.

In the game, the user plays as an immigration officer working at a border checkpoint for a fictitious Eastern European nation with tight foreign policy and hostile relations with its neighbors. The user's character has a wife, son, and other dependents, who quickly fall ill and die if the user doesn't bring home enough money at the end of each working day. The gamer must take or resist bribes from terror cells, decide whether to help threatened immigrants in need of asylum whose needs are officially rejected by the government, and consider whether to shoot, arrest, or join a whole host of different forces attempting to break or subvert governmental rule. The story immerses the player and forces the user to confront the difficult decision-making faced by those in such situations. The player must choose between upholding the law and keeping their family alive, and between breaking the law or sending refugees to their death. More organized subversion, such as involvement with anarchists, might help counter oppressive government but can put the family at risk, while accepting bribes from government officials might help pay the gas bill but causes disadvantaged citizens more suffering. *Papers, Please,* then, is a palpably ethical game, at least insofar as it forces the viewer to think about some of the issues involved in border control, immigration, and the everyday experience of working as a government employee: *The New Yorker,* for instance, noted that the game may "change your attitude" at the airport.[8] Yet the more subversive quality of *Papers, Please* is found somewhere else.

When a former immigration worker turns up with the wrong papers and is refused entry (if the user selects that option), he comments that now he "knows what it feels to be on the other side" and appeals to the gamer on the grounds that he should empathize with a man who previously occupied his own position of immigration officer. The former employee, however, makes this less about empathy and more about sadism and masochism, accusing the gamer of enjoying his use of the rejection stamp. There is pleasure for the worker too, not just in the irony of a border-control officer failing to cross a border but because the position of being subjected to the law seems nearly as enjoyable as the position of enforcing it. For Freud, "sadism and masochism occupy a special position among the perversions" because they involve the oscillating pleasure in moving from "activity to passivity," a movement at the center of sexual and pleasurable life (*SE 7*: 159). Elsewhere Freud makes a related comment, writing of playground games:

> As the child passes over from the passivity of the [lived] experience to the activity of the game, he hands on the disagreeable experience to one of his playmates and in this way revenges himself on a substitute.[9]

Defeat and passivity in the workplace can be "revenged" on the playmates in multiplayer gaming and even, via displacement, on the computer AI, making the passive and dissatisfied working subject avoid confronting his passivity in lived experience by replacing it with illusory activity and success in the videogame. Yet *Papers, Please* asks for yet more than this, showing how pleasure can be found in oscillating between active and passive. Many games speak to the desire for this sadomasochistic oscillation, most notably the recently popular "survival horror" genre whose most significant games may be *Outlast* (PC, PS4, 2015) and *Until Dawn* (PS4, 2015), and *Until Dawn: Rush of Blood* (PSVR, 2016). In these games, which form the dominant genre in the early days of PlayStation VR (see, for instance, *Kitchen,* 2016 and *Resident Evil: Biohazard,* 2017), the player is usually weaponless and passive, unable to do anything except run and hide, reversing the traditionally active pleasure of gaming.

This encounter with a former colleague in *Papers, Please* confronts the player with the realization that most of the gamer's own enjoyment has come not from the minor subversion of the authoritarian government's regulations and harsh employment and immigration laws, but from the regular and everyday imposition of the law onto the other. Further, it confronts the gamer with the realization that their own enjoyment is also found in the temporary imitation of the other. It also confronts the gamer with the realization that games can be pleasurable because they simulate the enforcement of the law. Where the typical view of such enjoyment considers the fun to be found in the fact that the police have exciting lives, this game reveals that pleasure comes not from a thrilling battle with the bad guys but from law enforcement *as such*, no matter how mundane and bureaucratic. It may show a Lacanian point that a perverse pleasure is derived from imposing the letter of the law, but it also doubles back on this by virtue of being a simulation of such pleasure, forcing the recognition. It shows that this kind of pleasure may have its roots in copying the pleasure of the other, of the former immigration officer, of the last gamer, of the law itself.

In opposite cases, most commonly AAA games with large funding packages, it is the subversive who is presented as the figure whose enjoyment the gamer is invited to experience. *Watchdogs*

(PS4, 2014–present) is the most prominent example of this. Its narrative celebrates subversive individuals such as Edward Snowden and Julian Assange by asking the gamer to idealize not the enjoyment of US army officers (e.g., *Call of Duty*) or misogynist Orient-plunderers (e.g., *Uncharted*), but the "enjoyment" of anti-establishment hackers. As such, the game appears ostensibly subversive, taking up a clear position against law-enforcing government and even "against capitalism." Whilst many games are based on the enjoyment of transgressive criminality, few focus on such organized methods of subversion. At the same time, however, the enjoyment derived from the game is structurally comparable to other videogames which offer identification with the imposition of the law. *Papers, Please* is a subversive game inviting the gamer to experience and reflect on conformist enjoyment, whereas *Watchdogs* is a conformist game inviting the gamer to experience subversive enjoyment without reflection.

All this forces the gamer to confront the fact that enjoyment may have no inherent connection to the object being enjoyed, nor to the person doing the enjoying, making a categorization of games (and of books, films, etc.) into subversive and non-subversive groups completely useless. Instead, enjoyment itself must be seen as something like a third object in a triangular relationship with reader and text, gamer and game, subject and object. It is entirely possible for subversive enjoyment to connect a conformist text with a conformist gamer, and it is equally likely that a self-confessed subversive can experience totally conformist enjoyment when engaging with a text they deem to be thoroughly "radical." Videogames, though increasingly part of the discourse of the next generation of potential subversives, remain predominantly in the realm of conformism, as argued above. As such, this is an important facet of their subversive potential. While the majority of producers and the majority of gamers approach the game with either conformist or apolitical attitudes, the enjoyment produced between subject and game can nevertheless be politically subversive. If this subversive potential of the dreamworld can be harnessed, it can be used to reach a wide and often initially unreceptive audience.

Jouissance in the Arcades

Perhaps this experience would be better conceptualized in relation to the proper Lacanian distinction between enjoyment (*jouissance*) and pleasure (*plaisir*). It is tempting to see pleasure as the less defined and perhaps more troubling of the two words, since it is usually applied to instinctive and sexual acts, whereas the word "enjoyment" is more often used to describe our relations with cultural objects, making it seem more structured, "cultivated," and perhaps easier to pin down or explain. On the contrary, however, Lacan insists upon enjoyment as the more troubling of the two, and argues that enjoyment should be seen as more primary. Whereas *jouissance* has no concern for the subject doing the enjoying, pleasure has a self-preserving instinct which reigns enjoyment in and "keeps you within a fairly buffered limit."[10] The best elucidation of the distinction is Aaron Schuster's:

> The logic of enjoyment is that of "too much" and "too little" without a "just right" – which is what pleasure is, except that this "just right" is never

really right enough, so one is soon tossed back into the unhappy turbulence of *jouissance*.

Pleasure should therefore be seen as limited or regulated *jouissance*, though this regulation is always failed, returning the subject to the troubling *jouissance* from whence it came. Insofar as the distinction can be maintained, we could ask whether videogames produce pleasure or enjoyment. However, it is hardly possible to ask the question this way, and Schuster also gives the best description of why:

> *Jouissance* is first and foremost a crisis; the psyche does not spontaneously know how to handle its own excitation and arousal, the drives put on the body under pressure, and the question is how and by what forces will this crisis be exploited: will it provoke a retrenchment of the ego's defenses, or can it be elaborated in a different direction?[11]

With this in mind, the dreamworld can be thought of as the world of *jouissance*. It involves unregulated pleasure and the breakdown of the order and sensibility of the pleasure principle, but it is also always simultaneously in the process of re-ordering and re-organizing. This can be put in the terms of Deleuze and Guattari, so often considered the opponents of psychoanalysis. Their neologisms "deterritorialization" and "reterritorialization" describe processes of breakdown which are always-already accompanied by forces of restructuring, and are not so far from the psychoanalytic relationship between *jouissance* and pleasure. In the dreamworld, the subject is put into crisis and under pressure, enjoying freely and madly, but there are always reterritorializing forces in play as well, pulling *jouissance* back to pleasure and ordering the subject in new ways.

The first page of this book compared the experience of entering the Playstation dreamworld with how it might feel to enter a Parisian arcade or a London department store in the mid-nineteenth century. It is of course no coincidence that since the 1970s gaming centers have taken their name from the arcades of the century before. Gaming is an experience of wish-fulfillment, reverie, and dreamlike hallucination that is thrilling, overwhelming, and intoxicating. In this book the aim has been to investigate what politics could be found inside this semi-conscious world full of commodities into which we escape, but where we are also formed and constructed, and a theory regarding what makes this experience possible and how it may operate on us as subjects has now been approached. The pace of technological development is rapid and the financial invest-ment in games, immersion, augmented reality, and VR is higher than ever. This new space, no longer a gaming arcade on the street but a virtual world that we can enter from anywhere, is highly enjoyable, both in the general sense and in the psychoanalytic one.

Walter Benjamin described how it felt to enter the arcades, writing that they were "a phantas-magoria in which primal history enters the scene in ultramodern get-up."[12] For Benjamin, the arcades were a dreamspace in which history col-lapses and in which new connections between past, present, and future are formed. The arcade is, in this sense, "a world of secret affinities."[13] The dreamworld, whether you enter through your phone, computer, handset, television, head-set, or goggles, is the modern incantation of this phantasmagoria in which history collapses and new relationships, connections, and affinities are formed, often secretly. Benjamin's com-ments about the arcades may also go some way to explaining the prevalence of nostalgia in the dreamworld, which, like the arcades, re-orders the subject in relation to history.

This space that provokes multiple forms of excessive and indefinable *jouissance* is a potentially dangerous one that threatens to throw the subject into crisis, a crisis from which the subject could at least potentially emerge in a different form. It is a case of asking Schuster's question of how this crisis will be exploited: will it provoke a retrenchment of the ego's defenses, or can it be elaborated in a different direction? From *Pokémon GO* to *Watchdogs,* from corporations to independent game designers, we are seeing a battle over this infinite new space, with various attempts to translate the endless *jouissance* of the dreamworld into pleasure that can function in the service of one ideology or another. The politics of this space and its pleasures are certainly worth fighting for.

Bonus Features

How To Be a Subversive Gamer

> Man has become a god by means of artifi-
> cial limbs, so to speak, quite magnificent
> when equipped with all his accessory
> organs; but they do not grow on him and
> they still give him trouble at times …
>
> Freud
> *Civilization and Its Discontents* (1929)

In 1987, with no experience in film-making
whatsoever, Felix Guattari sent a script for a mad
and bizarre sci-fi movie called *A Love of UIQ*
to France's National Center of Cinematography.
He attached his CV and hoped (probably
even believed) that it would go all the way to
Hollywood. Earlier in the decade, he even asked

the legendary director Michelangelo Antonioni to get involved with the project. Unsurprisingly, the film was never made. Had it been, it would have anticipated the questions faced by subjectivity in the age of gaming and ubiquitous digital communication. The screenplay provided a call for a machinic subjectivity that would combat the contemporary identity crises created by technological advances. This machinic subjectivity would finally achieve what Guattari had long hoped to do: render psychoanalysis – the tools used in this book - completely useless.

Nusselder's *Interface Fantasy* argued just the opposite. By bringing together psychoanalysis with the computer screen and making a new case for "updating" Lacanian ideas of fantasy in the context of ICT, Nusselder showed how psychoanalytic theory could be seen as more necessary than ever in the digital age.[1] Even so, psychoanalysis has not been as influential in discussions of technology as have the ideas of Deleuze and Guattari, who are responsible for what remains the most compelling critique of psychoanalysis to date. Indeed, Guattari's criticism continues to insist, making its presence felt even as the psychoanalysis of people and things goes on: do the

Lacanian models still apply to the subjects of today and will they apply to the subjects of the future? This book hopes to have shown that psychoanalysis is a vital framework for discussions of technology. In this enjoyment-oriented society, the politics and technics of enjoyment are made visible by a psychoanalytic approach. At the same time, if psychoanalysis is to speak not to "universal human truths" but to historical and cultural formations of subjectivity, then the mutation and evolution of subjectivity discussed in this book means that psychoanalysis must change to confront the cyborgs to come.

Though Guattari's texts have received more attention in recent years, for most people he is still, first and foremost, Deleuze's friend. Perhaps best embodied by Andrew Culp's *Dark Deleuze*, critics have recovered Deleuze from those who saw him as the philosopher of "joyous affirmation" and who experienced his work (often without admitting it) as vitalist, life-affirming, and positive. Such readings brought Deleuze onto the side of puritanical pro-lifers, feel-good self-help fanatics, manic shopaholics, and hippy free-spirits.[2] Instead, readings like Culp's have shown the "dark side" of Deleuze: his negativity, his resistance to all things celebratory of nature, impulse and freedom, and ultimately his embrace of "death." This argument is not just academic bickering about Deleuze but a vital argument about our politics going forward in the techno-logical age. It hinges on the difference between those technophiles who continue to seek expe-riences which are free of or combative against technological power, and those who feel that there is no way back to an untechnological expe-rience and who embrace the kind of death of the human that would be (or has been) heralded by our becoming machine. *A Love of UIQ* has been used here because it shows Guattari on this dark side of Deleuze, and because it raises the power-ful question of whether psychoanalysis will work on a machinic subjectivity which – this book has argued – is already here.

Shaviro argues that in the world of genetic engi-neering and Big Data, the opposition between nature and culture is unsustainable and that we need to recognize that nature is "always in move-ment, in process and under construction" socially and culturally, never "outside history" but deter-mined by it.[3] The nature of our consciousness is changed by our relationship to machines and technology. For Berardi, who goes further in exploring the precise changes in consciousness that occur in the technological age, the digital infosphere and the age of hyperconnectivity change the cognitive model, affecting "aesthetic sensibility" and "emotional sensitivity."[4] Such ideas have been explored here in relation to the effects of videogaming, which plays a key role in such transformations. An attempt has been made to explore the politics of these changes, thinking through the ways in which gaming creates new possibilities for empathy, identification, impulse, and desire. The focus has been on who is taking advantage of this potential and to what ends they are working.

We read in Guattari's script that *A Love of UIQ* is about finding "a machinic subjectivity – hyper-intelligent and yet infantile and regressive [...] that has no fixed limits and no clear psychological or sexual orientation." In short, this machinic consciousness is a subjectivity which – for want of a better term – is "free" of the organizing principles of traditional human identity. In other words, it is a subjectivity without boundaries, physical, spatial, or conceptual. This "UIQ" represents a deterritorialized subject, a subject which can transgress boundaries, which is prior to or without sexual orientation, and which escapes those arboreal and structured subjectivities confining the humans in the movie. The gamer may be just such a subject today, deterritorialized but awaiting reterritorialization.

Perhaps the greatest clue that the subjectivity of UIQ is conceived of as a response to psychoanalysis comes in the key line:

> This is like fucking Nobel-Prize incredible. The discovery of the century! A language! I mean … something like a language, that comes from the very depths of cellular life![5]

As well as mocking the self-indulgent idea that psychoanalysis could be comparable to the discoveries of Marie Curie (referred to elsewhere in the script), the passage directly invokes a comment by Lacan, who said that "the unconscious is structured like a language" and that "it speaks." Guattari is parodying the idea, constructing a fictional reality in which a kind of unconscious force is structured like a language, and, literally, speaks to humans. In the earlier *The Machinic Unconscious* (1979) Guattari had mocked this

Lacanian idea, and here he takes the parody further by humorously exploring what it would be like if the unconscious could have a full chat with people.

Eventually, the UIQ begins to develop human emotions and falls in love with a real person, the punk Janice, who has taught the UIQ about human identity, sexuality, and a sense of "self". The message of this transformation is that the machinic deterritorialized subjectivity that is the UIQ, previously free from the boundaries and restrictions imposed by identity in the human world, now becomes human-like, reterritorializing to acquire a sexuality, a gender (it even becomes a "he" in the script), and a full set of human desires. In short, the UIQ becomes the structural subjectivity embodied by Guattari's reading of psychoanalysis. Rather than "a desiring machine," the UIQ is transformed into a heterosexual male in love with Janice as the lacking object of desire, and becomes desperately susceptible to fits of jealous rage when she speaks to other men. For Guattari, it would be a terrible shame to become the subject that Lacan described, if there was another option.

In an unusual way, the screenplay looks

forward to recent films such as Spike Jonze's *Her* (2013) and Alex Garland's *Ex Machina* (2015), both of which envisage the human subject falling in love with a computer. This reading is much indebted to Srećko Horvat, who remarks that what we are dealing with in such instances is not so much falling in love with a machine but falling narcissistically in love with yourself as you are reflected back to yourself in the "other" via the computer. However, in *A Love of UIQ* the situation is reversed: UIQ, the computer consciousness, learning human emotions, falls in love with a human. Thus, whilst the message of films such as *Ex Machina* may be like Horvat's argument in *The Radicality of Love,* that even the deepest human emotions are now automated by technological forces which organize and control our impulses and desires, Guattari's script involves both this and the reverse: that whilst our deepest desires may become automated, the computer's deepest desires may become human.[6] This, for Guattari, would be the true tragedy: not the loss of human identity as we become machine but the loss of a machinic alternative to it as we become human. Thus, the "film" plays on a well-trodden sci-fi fear that computers could develop consciousness. What makes this idea unsettling in most sci-fi movies is that if computers can gain that "special something" that makes us human, the unique status of what it means to be human would be destroyed. On the contrary, what makes the computer's transformation into the human tragic in Guattari's film is the reverse: the tragedy is that if the computer becomes human, then the machinic potentiality for new subjectivities is destroyed.

A Love of UIQ, then, is not about humans becoming mere machines but about machines becoming mere humans. We can easily think of machines becoming human in 2017, from developments in robotics that are increasingly obsessed with human replicas through to the everyday encounters we have with the personality of Siri (Apple's intelligent personal assistant and knowledge navigator) and Cortana (the Microsoft equivalent). Evidence is even found in the new features of Facebook, which has begun to wish us "Good morning" and converse with us in chatty language about our friends' birthdays.[7] Perhaps Silicon Valley is turning our machines into humans to avoid them becoming troubling Guattarian subjects. The catastrophe, from a

Guattarian point of view, is not that we would become machine but that we would miss the opportunity to do so.

In this way, *A Love of UIQ* could make a contribution to the seemingly endless discussions of Deleuze vs Lacan. It shows the need for Deleuze and Guattari's challenge to psychoanalysis, revealing to us that psychoanalysis did not anticipate a machinic potentiality for the subject to be other than the lacking subject that psychoanalysis knows so well. It also shows that their rejection of psychoanalysis came too soon, and perhaps that we are still not ready for it, since it may take the transformation into machine and the death of the human to move beyond the psychoanalytic subject. It may be some time then, before psychoanalysis is not needed, but it certainly poses a challenge to the status of psychoanalysis in the machinic age to come.

What this book hopes to have shown is that developments in videogames, mobile-phone games, virtual reality, and entertaining technology mean that psychoanalysis is needed more than ever, but that it is needed in a different way. It is needed to unseat something that psychoanalysis is itself often paradoxically accused of and has at times been guilty of: investing in desires that are not political and in a structure of subjectivity that cannot be changed. Instead, in a society in which technology and entertainment are inseparable and ubiquitous, a psychoanalysis of technology makes the new politics of desire, enjoyment, and pleasure visible to us. This kind of understanding must be the first step toward changing a world in which subjectivity is – whether we like it or not – being mutated by technological change.

The Xenofeminism collective asks why there is so little "explicit, organized effort to repurpose technologies for progressive gender political ends," and seeks to "strategically deploy existing technologies to re-engineer the world."[8] The #ACCELERATE manifesto, despite Benjamin Noys' fantastic critique of accelerationism, has done something similar for Marxism. Unlike Marxism and feminism, psychoanalysis has a reputation for being the slowest and least changeable of theoretical approaches. On the contrary, I hope to have shown here that a psychoanalysis for the future and for technology can be developed and is vital alongside Marxism and feminism. I have argued that anyone with subversive intentions needs to work inside cyberspace, rather than

siding with exclusionism and isolationism or falling into technophilia. In the attempt to fight the
corporate and state control of cyberspace, the job
of today's philosophers of technology must be to
lay the theoretical groundwork for the next generation of educated but angry people who know
how to use and reprogram technology in a way
that the previous generation do not. Optimism
can be found in the fact that corporate and state
organizations will no longer be able to absorb the
majority of those capable of using technology to
the highest level. It should at least be clear that the
separation between philosophy and technology
has been deliberate and has served a combina-
tion of increasingly inseparable corporate and
state interests. Philosophy and technology must
become one and the same again. Here I have used
psychoanalysis to make visible some hidden technological patterns in the hope of contributing to
this groundwork.

The "gamer" should no longer be regarded as a
term implying a certain "alternative" identity as it
did in the saga of Gamergate. Instead, it describes
an increasingly large portion of the global population. The saturation rate of console, online, and
mobile games is so high that such technologies

are forming the current generation and the next. If we take entertainment applications as implicated in the same patterns (is *Pokémon GO* so different from Tinder?), then we can extend the reach of such technologies to include nearly all of the world's online population, a rising figure already well over 3 billion. This new "gamer" has the kind of machinic potential for a new subjectivity described by Guattari. At the same time as signaling massive opportunity for change, this poses a huge danger, increasing the ability of state and corporate actors to organize these new subjects and their pathologies. It is now a question of responding without technophilia or technophobia and of working out precisely how to influence machinic subjectivities to mobilize against these corporate forces.

Credits

Tutorial: The Pokémon Generation

1   Gilles Deleuze, *Foucault,* trans. Sean Hand (Minnesota, MN: University of Minnesota Press, 2006), p. 39.
2   Donna Haraway, "A Cyborg Manifesto," in *Simians, Cyborgs and Women: The Reinvention of Nature* (New York: Routledge, 1991), pp. 149–81 (p. 151).
3   McKenzie Wark, *Gamer Theory* (Cambridge, MA: Harvard University Press, 2007), section 006.
4   Steven Shaviro, *No Speed Limit: Three Essays on Accelerationism* (Minneapolis, MN: University of Minnesota Press, 2014), p. 10.
5   See Srećko Horvat with Alfie Bown, *Advancing Conversations: Subversion!* (Washington and Winchester: Zero Books, 2017).
6   Julian Assange, *When Google Met WikiLeaks* (New York: OR Books, 2014).
7   For a further treatment of mapping APIs, see

Alfie Bown, "Algorithmic Control and the Revolution of Desire," in *ROAR Magazine* 4 (winter 2016): 90–9.

8 Guy Debord, "The Theory of the Dérive," in Ken Knabb (ed.), *Situationist International Anthology* (Berkeley, CA: Bureau of Public Secrets, 1981), pp. 50–4.

9 Jacques Lacan, *Seminar II: The Ego in Freud's Theory and in the Technique of Psychoanalysis, 1954–1955*, ed. Jacques-Alain Miller (London: W.W. Norton: 1991), pp. 223–4.

11 Sigmund Freud, "The 'Uncanny'," in *The Standard Edition of the Complete Psychological Works of Sigmund Freud, Volume XVII (1917–1919): An Infantile Neurosis and Other Works*, ed. and trans. James Strachey (London: Vintage, 2001), pp. 217–56 (p. 249).

11 Yuk Hui, *On the Existence of Digital Objects* (Minnesota, MN: University of Minnesota Press, 2016), p. 3.

12 Srećko Horvat, *The Radicality of Love* (Cambridge: Polity, 2015).

13 See Jean-François Lyotard, "Desirevolution," in Robin Mackay and Armen Avanessian (eds), *#ACCELERATE: The Accelerationist Reader* (Falmouth: Urbanomic, 2014), pp. 241–50.

14 Sam Kriss, "Resist Pokémon Go," found at: <https://www.jacobinmag.com/2016/07/pokemon-go-poke stops-game-situationist-play-children/>.

15 Franco "Bifo" Berardi, "The Summer of Pokémon Go," found at: < https://diem25.org/the-summer-of-pokemon-go/>.

Level 1 From Farming Simulation to Dystopic Wasteland: Gaming and Capitalism

1 E. M. Forster, *The Machine Stops* (New York: Start Classics, 2012), p. 6.

2 For the full breadth of this argument, see Alfie Bown, *Enjoying It: Candy Crush and Capitalism* (Winchester and Washington: Zero Books, 2015), pp. 1–5.

3 E. P. Thompson, *The Making of the English Working Class* (Harmondsworth: Penguin, 1968), p. 898.

4 Jane McGonigal, *Reality is Broken* (London: Vintage Books, 2012), p. 53.

5 Ibid., p. 346.

6 Ibid., p. 349.

7 Alberto Posso, "Internet Usage and Educational Outcomes Among 15-Year-Old Australian Students," in *International Journal of Communication* 10 (2016): 3851–76.

8 Siegfried Kracauer, *The Mass Ornament,* trans. Thomas Y. Levin (Cambridge, MA: Harvard University Press, 1988), pp. 91–6.

9 Svetlana Boym, *The Future of Nostalgia* (New York: Basic Books, 2002), p. xiv.

10 Dominic Pettman, *Infinite Distraction* (Cambridge: Polity, 2016), p. 11.

11 Mark Fisher, "The Great Digital Swindle," found at: <http://repeaterbooks.com/extracts/the-great-digital-swindle/>.

12 Jeffrey Tam, "Fallout: Why Don't We Set the World on Fire," found at <http://existentialgamer.com/fallout-set-world-on-fire>.

13 I owe this point to Kimberley Clarke.
14 The very same logic underlies the second game by the same company, *Transistor* (PC, 2014), even though the game ostensibly presents itself as the opposite embrace of technological future.
15 Espen Aarseth, "Allegories of Space: The Question of Spatiality in Computer Games," in *Cybertext Yearbook 2000,* ed. Markku Eskelinen and Raine Koskimaa (Finland: Research Centre for Contemporary Culture, 2001), pp. 152–71.
16 Yanis Varoufakis, "A Day of Victory for the Politics of Fear, Loathing and Division," found at: <https://diem25.org/trumps-triumph-how-progressives-must-react/>.
17 Quoted in Walter Benjamin, *Selected Writings Volume 3: 1935–1938,* ed. Edward Jephcott and Howard Eiland (Cambridge, MA: Harvard University Press, 2002), p. 33.

Level 2   Dreamwork: Cyborgs on the Analyst's Couch

1 Ian Bogost, *How to Talk about Videogames* (London: University of Minnesota Press, 2015), p. 1.
2 Sigmund Freud, *The Standard Edition of the Complete Psychological Works of Sigmund Freud, Volume XV: Introductory Letters on Psycho-analysis*, ed. and trans. James Strachey (London: Vintage, 2001), p. 136.
3 Jacques Lacan, *The Four Fundamental Concepts of Psychoanalysis: The Seminar of Jacques Lacan Book XI,* ed. Jacques-Alain Miller, trans. Alan Sheridan (London: W. W. Norton, 1998), p. 49.

4 Sigmund Freud, "The Interpretation of Dreams," in *The Standard Edition of the Complete Psychological Works of Sigmund Freud, Volume 5,* ed. and trans. James Strachey (London: Vintage, 2001), p. 218.

5 If the gamer plays for long enough, *Cookie Clicker* envisages the collapse of capitalism from within, giving it a final subversive message that the majority of its players never see.

6 Robert Pfaller, *On the Pleasure Principle in Culture: Illusions Without Owners* (London: Verso, 2014) p. 177.

7 Slavoj Žižek, *The Sublime Object of Ideology* (London: Verso, 1989), p. 94.

8 After writing this section I learned that I was not the first to discuss the relationship between the philosophical concept of *dromena* and videogames. The connection was first made by Alexander R. Galloway, who makes a different argument using the concept. See *Gaming: Essays on Algorithmic Culture* (Minnesota, MN: University of Minnesota Press, 2006), pp. 19–25.

9 Edwin Montoya Zorrilla, "VR and the Empathy Machine," in *The Hong Kong Review of Books* (December, 2016), available at: <https://hkrbooks.com/2016/07 / 22 / hkrb - essays - pokemon - go - and - the - enigma - of -the-city/>.

10 André Nusselder, *Interface Fantasy: A Lacanian Cyborg Ontology* (Cambridge, MA: MIT Press, 2009). p. 11.

11 Ernest Cline, *Ready Player One* (London: Arrow Books, 2012), pp. 57, 60.

12 Ibid., p. 171.

Level 3   Retro Gaming: The Politics of Former and Future Pleasures

1 Grafton Tanner, *Babbling Corpse: Vaporwave and the Commodification of Ghosts* (Winchester and Washington: Zero Books, 2017), pp. 1–13.

2 Mark Fisher, *Ghosts of My Life: Writings on Depression, Hauntology and Lost Futures* (Winchester and Washington: Zero Books, 2014), p. 2.

3 Michael McWhertor, "Which Legend of Zelda Game Was Inspired by Twin Peaks?," found at: <http://kotaku.com/5457701/which-legend-of-zelda-game-was-inspired-by-twin-peaks>.

4 Jean-Luc Nancy, *The Sense of the World*, trans. Jeffrey S. Librett (Minneapolis, MN: University of Minnesota Press, 1997). p. 47.

5 Slavoj Žižek, in *The Pervert's Guide to Cinema*, dir. Sophie Fiennes (UK: Mischief Films, 2006).

6 D. Fox Harrell and Sneha Veeragoudar Harrell, "Imagination, Computation, and Self-Expression: Situated Character and Avatar Mediated Identity," in *Leonardo Electronic Almanac: After Media: Embodiment and Context* 17/2 (January 2012): 74–91 (p. 89). Fox Harrell's major book on the subject is *Phantasmal Media: An Approach to Imagination, Computation, and Expression* (Cambridge. MA: MIT Press, 2013).

7 Bob Rehack, "Playing at Being: Psychoanalysis and the Avatar," in Judith Butler (ed.), *Excitable Speech: A Politics of the Performative* (London: Routledge, 2013), pp. 103–8 (pp. 105–7).

8   Simon Parkin, "The Best Videogames of 2013," available at: <http://www.newyorker.com/tech/elements/the-best-video-games-of-2013>.

9   Sigmund Freud, "Beyond the Pleasure Principle," in *The Standard Edition of the Complete Psychological Works of Sigmund Freud Vol 18*, ed. and trans. James Strachey (London: Vintage, 2001), pp. 7–64 (p. 17).

10 Jacques Lacan, "Seminar XIV: The Logic of Fantasy," session of June 14, 1967 (unpublished).

11 Aaron Schuster, *The Trouble with Pleasure: Deleuze and Psychoanalysis* (Cambridge, MA: MIT Press, 2016), pp. 118–19.

12 Walter Benjamin, "Arcades II," in *The Arcades Project*, trans. Rolf Tiedemann (Cambridge, MA: Harvard University Press, 1999) pp. 873–84 (p. 874).

13 Walter Benjamin, *The Arcades Project*, p. 116.

Bonus Features: How To Be a Subversive Gamer

1   Andre Nusselder, *Interface Fantasy: A Lacanian Cyborg Ontology* (Cambridge, MA: MIT Press, 2009).

2   Andrew Culp, *Dark Deleuze* (Minnesota, MN: University of Minnesota Press, 2016).

3   Steven Shaviro, *Discognition* (London: Repeater Books, 2016), pp. 222–3.

4   Franco "Bifo" Berardi, *And: The Phenomenology of the End* (London: Semiotexte, 2026), p. 11.

5   Felix Guattari, *A Love of UIQ*, trans. Silvia Maglioni and Graeme Thompson (Minneapolis, MN: Univocal, 2016), p. 97.

6　See Srećko Horvat, *The Radicality of Love,* pp. 23–41.
7　For an example of videogames which reflect on these social media issues, see *Life is Strange* (PS4, 2015).
8　See <http://www.laboriacuboniks.net/>.

Game Index

GAME INDEX